REA

**DO NOT REMOVE
CARDS FROM POCKET**

SCHOOL SAVVY

*Everything You Need to
Know to Guide Your Child
Through Today's Schools*

DIANE HARRINGTON
AND LAURETTE YOUNG

THE NOONDAY PRESS
FARRAR, STRAUS AND GIROUX
New York

Library of Congress Cataloging-in-Publication Data

Harrington, Diane.
School savvy : everything you need to know to
guide your child through today's schools /
Diane Harrington and Laurette Young.—1st ed.
p.   cm.
Includes bibliographical references.
1. Education—United States—Parent participation.   2. Home and
school—United States.   I. Young, Laurette.   II. Title.
LB1048.5.H37 1993   370.19′31—dc20   93-10943   CIP

To our families and friends

CONTENTS

INTRODUCTION

The germs of our passion for parent participation began many years ago. For Laurette, it started in the spring of 1979 when she volunteered to type a collection of children's writings for her daughter's elementary school PTA. She had one of those typewriters with changeable fonts—very high tech for that time. One thing led to another, and she found herself editing the PTA newsletter the next year. "If you're writing a newsletter, you have to go to Board of Education meetings and PTA meetings, interview people, and find out enough information to write believable articles about different issues. I had to research everything!" Laurette recalls. By September 1980, she was president of the PTA, and she has never looked back.

For Diane, it began when her daughter entered kindergarten in 1987. New to the neighborhood, she didn't know a soul. And the school didn't help her: There was no handbook and no communication about school routines. She wanted to know the simple things—like what happened when kids got off their buses and what to do when it snowed in the morning—but she didn't know whom to ask. To meet people and find out what was what, she went to PTA meetings, where she asked questions and volunteered to help: "Could we do a handbook for parents?" "Could we parents help escort kindergartners to their classrooms for a while?" The school's new principal appreciated Diane's questions where others hadn't and invited her to join the principal's advisory committee. Here her questions were welcomed and discussed.

For both of us, then, the desire for more information sparked our participation. And that is probably what has brought you to our book.

You might be reading this because your child is about to enter kindergarten, or perhaps you're moving to a new town with unfamiliar schools. It might be that your school district gives you a choice of schools for your child, or maybe you are researching the local schools as a consumer and a taxpayer. Perhaps your motivation is that your child has been experiencing some difficulties in school, or you think your child has some special needs. No matter which of these reasons is yours, you might be feeling anxious because you want to make the "right" decisions—those that will help your child succeed in school.

The first thing we want you to know is that this is not a recipe book. We don't have easy answers to guide you through the choices confronting you or to help you deal with your child's daily ups and downs at school. No one does. Our advice comes from real-life experiences; the strategies we share have worked for us and for other parents we know. But your knowledge of your child and your parenting and observation skills are the most reliable signposts to help you sort among these strategies.

Our book offers much more than advice, however practical and appealing that might be. In many instances, we raise questions as well as try to provide some answers. Because close observation of your child is one way for you to find your own answers, we give tips throughout the book on what to look for and how to do it. Where we think it's needed, we also provide background information on key subjects. We encourage you to dig deeper and find out more—and especially to question the decisions made for and by your child. And we urge you to do so in partnership with the school as much as you can.

We believe that all parents, even busy parents like us, can and should take part in their children's educational lives. If you're reading this, you probably agree. But what isn't always self-evident is *how* and *when* to get involved. We hope our book will help you choose to influence and support your child's school experience in ways that are most appropriate for you and your family.

Although the stories we tell are based on fact, we've changed some of the details and all of the names to protect the privacy of the parents and schoolpeople from many communities who shared their experiences with us.

SCHOOL SAVVY

1

GETTING INVOLVED

Schoolpeople say they want parents to be involved in their children's education. Parents say they want to participate. And yet, all too often, the connections just aren't made. So what's the problem? For one thing, everyone has different ideas about what parent participation should entail. Moreover, it scares some schoolpeople—those who believe that parents will take over the schools if they get too involved. And it intimidates busy parents who feel it is the schools' responsibility—not theirs—to educate their children.

In this chapter we present what we call the *parent participation continuum*—a range of roles and levels within those roles for taking part in your child's education. It starts with the most basic level of parent support and ends with examples of parent activism.

Believe it or not, academic researchers have conducted literally hundreds of studies to confirm what we parents already knew: Children of parents who are involved in their education demonstrate a higher level of academic achievement than children whose parents are not. This holds true in all types of communities: rich and poor, black and white, Asian and Latino, and every other group you can think of. *Involved parents mean more successful children.* It's that simple!

In addition, the research cites other, less dramatic payoffs for students, schools, and parents. Increased self-esteem, fewer behavior problems, and improved school attendance are noticeable in children of involved parents. Parents become more effective and more self-confident because of their participation. Schools are winners, too, through the rich resources that parents bring and the support that involved parents generate. Parental input results in programs that are more sensitive to individual children's needs. In addition, by being in the school more often and becoming known to school personnel, parents are better able to hold schools accountable.

Every time we speak up, ask a question, or intervene for our children, we're helping other children, too. What we want for *our* children in school—a secure, nurturing, and challenging environment—is what all parents want, even those who never speak up. When we make our voices heard, we help to create that kind of environment for all children.

We've listed dozens of ways you can be involved. You can choose those that suit your family best. Whether your family is headed by two parents or one, whether you work in the home or outside it, whether you are affluent or struggling to make ends meet, you will find appropriate ways to take part in your child's schooling.

We both consider ourselves "involved" parents, yet we have taken quite different routes. Your involvement, like ours, must be custom-tailored to your child's needs and your own circumstances. It might change over time as your child gets older, as your own interests and circumstances evolve, or as difficulties emerge in school or at home. There is no magic formula.

PARENTS AS SUPPORTERS

Providing basic support for our children's education is the first station on the parent participation continuum. It includes the necessities of life—those things we parents provide automatically for our children, such as love, food, and shelter. But even more important are the ways in which we create the conditions that enable our children to learn. Some of this support is quite easy to provide and takes little or no time, while other activities require a bit more effort.

• *Read, read, read—to and with your child.* Experts agree that nothing is more essential to school success than solid reading skills, and these are buttressed by reading at home. Read to your child at bedtime; read side by side on the couch after dinner; read signs aloud on the road or titles on TV or labels on soup cans. Read whenever and wherever you can. Your child will be a better reader as a result.

• *Establish routines for meals, bedtime, study time.* Studies have shown that children with well-defined routines at home have an easier time adapting to school routines. (By routines we mean consistent times, places, and rules—no TV during dinner, for example—that help to make a child's life predictable.) These routines demonstrate an expectation that there is "a time and a place for everything." We know, your parents probably said that to you many years ago; so did ours. They were right.

In busy families, this might not be easy to do every night of the week. It is important, though, for parents to make a strong effort to keep to a routine. It pays off in the long run.

• *Give your child responsibility for chores at home.* Children who are responsible for small jobs around the house—setting or clearing the table, walking the dog, cleaning up after playing with Legos—are better prepared to handle the increasing responsibility expected by their teachers.

• *Make sure your child attends school regularly and gets there on time.* This gives the message that you value school and that you expect your child to take his school responsibilities seriously. Sometimes you might want to let your child take the day off if she is feeling pressured; but this should be a very rare exception.

• *Model respect for the school and teacher.* When you promote good attendance, insist upon high standards for homework, show up for parent-teacher conferences on time, and talk regularly about school activities, you demonstrate your own respect for the school and teacher. This tells your child that you value his hard work and his time there, that these are important responsibilities.

This isn't always easy. We've been challenged many times to bite our tongues in the face of bad decisions and inappropriate behavior by schoolpeople. And so have our friends. One told us about this comment made by a fourth-grade teacher in front of the class: "Katie, what a lovely haircut you have!" (Katie was smiling when the bombshell came.) "But maybe you want to ask your mother what you should do about that dandruff." Katie came home devastated. Her mom, instead of calling names, helped Katie understand that the tactless teacher was trying to be helpful.

• *Supervise your child's homework.* Set aside a certain time and place for homework—on the kitchen table while you're fixing dinner, for example—that's comfortable for your child and you. Establish appropriate rules, such as no TV or phone calls, then stick to all these conditions. They will ease the trials and tribulations of homework. (We'll talk more about homework later. Because it is a struggle for so many of us, we've devoted a whole chapter to it.)

• *Display your child's work.* A large assortment of refrigerator magnets is indispensable in our households. We use these to display on the refrigerator door special pieces of artwork, tests, or any papers our children think are important. These don't have to be *A* papers; sometimes our children's best is a *B* or *B* − . By putting this work up, we are celebrating the effort that went into it.

During the school year, at least two or three items per child are always on display in our homes, giving our kids the message that we think their work is special enough to show off.

• *Encourage your child to complete her work on time.* This is a hard one; it will take a bit of effort on your part, especially as your child gets older. One of us has found that a monthly calendar on the refrigerator is a good place for keeping track of due dates for long-term assignments such as book reports and research papers. We all know how many times the refrigerator is opened every day.

• *Communicate high expectations for your child.* Encourage your child to do her best in everything she does, from playing the flute to doing her homework. By doing so, you give the clear message that you expect her to do well.

• *Help your child learn to accept mistakes.* Making mistakes is part of the learning process. Help your child learn from his mistakes instead of being embarrassed or discouraged by them. A girl we know was so afraid of failing that she wouldn't try anything new. She was dying to learn to use the computer but gave up in tears each time she made a mistake. Her mom's solution was to sign the two of them up for a computer course together.

When they're young, our children don't think of us as ever making mistakes. It can be helpful to point out your own mistakes so they see that even a competent adult doesn't do everything right all the time. Talk with your child about solutions. A child who can turn his mistakes to his advantage will be a confident learner.

Supporting your child's learning doesn't take place only at home; that's also what you're doing when you volunteer to help the school or teacher in these ways:

• *Participate in school or PTA fund-raisers.* There's hardly a school anywhere in America that doesn't hold book fairs or bake sales or family feasts to raise money. And none of these events can take place without volunteers. Even if you work all day, as we do, there are ways you can help. You can buy (or bake) cupcakes; you might be able to go to work late one morning, after helping to sell books for an hour or two; you can certainly make phone calls in the evening; you can be a chaperone at a Friday night roller-skating party; or you can make decorations for the Valentine's Day dance.

• *Offer to help the teacher.* Even if you work outside the home or are confined by an infant, there are many ways you can help to cut down the noninstructional demands made on your child's teacher. Offer to type the monthly parent newsletter. Call other parents in the evening to arrange a class party. Help to plan the itinerary for a field trip. Visit the library on Saturdays to locate needed books. A little extra time on your part can mean a little extra attention for a child. And it tells your child that you and the teacher are partners.

• *Volunteer in other areas of the school.* Perhaps the library could use a story teller or an extra pair of hands at the circulation desk. Or maybe the nurse isn't at the school full-time. A mom we know covered the nurse's office every other Friday. Usually it was pretty boring, but one week while she was there she helped a boy with a broken arm. You might be able to help out in the main office, too. Volunteers are needed throughout most schools, which are always understaffed.

PARENTS AS AUDIENCE

One of the most devastating things that could happen to an actor is for no one to show up for his performance. In a way our children are like actors. They learn their spelling words, practice their parts in a school play, or work hard preparing oral reports for social studies. It is hard for them not to feel crushed when we say we're too busy to listen to them. Here are some ways even the busiest parent can be an appreciative audience:

• *Listen to your child—really listen.* Try not to ask your child questions such as, "What happened at school today?" Instead, ask open-ended ones that encourage *real* conversation and that will inform you about the day's happenings, such as: "What's one interesting thing you learned in school today?" "What kind of things do you like about the book you're reading?"

Listen to your child's responses. As we point out later, her answers to these kinds of questions will provide you with a lot of information about her academic and social life.

• *Be your child's audience at home.* At the end of a long,

hard day, the last thing a parent wants to do is listen to a
list of spelling words or hear a report on the jungles of
Brazil. But it is important for you to be your child's audience when you can. Besides the obvious message that you
care, it also tells your child that you believe education is
so important, you are willing to adjust your schedule to
help him with his schoolwork.

You might have to make some tradeoffs—no Thursday
night gourmet dinners (are there parents out there who still
make five-course dinners?) so you'll have time to quiz your
child for the weekly current events test on Friday. Refer
frequently to the calendar where you've noted the due dates
of your child's assignments and tests. This will help you
budget your time so that you can be available when your
child needs your assistance.

• *Attend school functions.* At the beginning of the year, the
school or the PTA lets parents know the dates of special
school events—back-to-school night, fall or spring music
concert, book fair, parent organization meetings, to name
just a few. We have found that the only way to remember
these events is to mark them on a calendar immediately.
Again, your attendance conveys the message that you support your child and the school and appreciate the time and
effort that goes into each event.

• *Attend family events at the school.* One of our schools
holds annual back-to-school and end-of-the-year picnics.
Others offer family fun nights, Saturday trips to a museum,
read-a-thons or game nights, or Friday night skating parties. If you go, you'll have an opportunity to meet your
child's friends and their families, and you'll get to see the
school staff in a different setting.

PARENTS AS LEARNERS

Our learning, as it relates to our children's education, equips us to support our children, advocate for them, understand and collaborate on decisions affecting them, and become decision makers in their schools or school districts. Here are some things you can do:

• *Join the parents' association.* Almost every school in the country has a parents' association. Hundreds of them, in fact, are part of the national PTA and include teachers in their membership. Often stereotyped as a group of women baking cookies and serving tea, present-day PTAs do much more. They provide support groups for parents and teachers, sponsor workshops on educational and child development issues, help fund assemblies and field trips the schools might not be able to afford, lobby for legislative changes, and provide a forum for parents to voice their concerns. In New York State, for example, the present law requiring seat belts on all school buses was the result of intensive PTA lobbying.

If you find the PTA in your child's school a closed group or if you're dissatisfied with its activities (too much cookies and tea perhaps), it's even more crucial for you to join. In most schools, this is the only forum for parents. Only by paying dues and raising your voice can you change the organization.

• *Attend school board meetings.* The board frequently invites staff to make presentations about curriculum or programs at these meetings. The knowledge you gain will help you support your child and be more informed if you have the opportunity to vote on the school budget.

• *Attend PTA meetings and other workshops and confer-*

ences open to parents. You'll learn more about the school and district people and programs by attending these events. You can find out about them from the PTA newsletter and bulletin board, district newsletters or flyers, and other parents.

• *Participate in school staff development activities.* Recently our schools have begun to invite parents to participate in a few staff development courses. Some topics useful to parents might be stress reduction, decision making, and consensus building. Find out what your school district has to offer, and sign up. You'll get a different perspective of school staff when you sit around a table with them.

• *Attend "make and take" workshops.* These fun events for parents and children are designed to reinforce a subject taught in school, to show parents ways to support their children's learning at home, or to introduce new educational concepts. Family Math is a popular workshop series that shows parents how to have fun at home with their children while reinforcing basic math skills.

At one workshop we know about, first-grade teachers, hoping to emphasize the message that "reading is important," help parents and children produce their own big books from materials found in everyone's home. The completed books then become part of the home library.

• *Read everything sent home from your child's school or district.* Sometimes school/district/PTA newsletters become our bedtime reading. Not exactly what you want to curl up with? We understand and agree, but it's important to be well informed.

• *Join a support group.* Our district has formed support groups for parents of children with handicaps, minor learning problems, or intellectual gifts. In addition, support groups for grandmothers raising their grandchildren and for single parents have been offered—sometimes in conjunction with the PTA. If your school has a parent support group relevant to you, think about joining it. If it doesn't, you might want to start one.

A few years ago, Laurette began a support group to talk about living with teenagers. First she approached the school, which was very sympathetic and was able to provide space once a week. Then she found a parent who was a social worker and was willing to be group leader. Finally the school sent home a flyer to all parents. The group met weekly for months, and the regular participants found it helped them get through their children's adolescence.

• *Learn about the school's expectations and requirements.* You have lots of sources for this: other parents, the school handbook, the district calendar, the teacher, and PTA officers, to name a few. Some of the things you'll learn are what happens when your child gets sick in school, how to report your child's absence, how to find out when school is closed for bad weather, and what happens when your child forgets her lunch. Both you and your child will feel more secure about school when you understand these routines.

• *Learn what your options are.* A small but growing number of school districts offer parents the opportunity to choose their children's school. Sometimes the choice is only at a certain level, such as elementary or junior high. Sometimes there are only one or two "schools of choice" (usually called "magnet schools"). These often have a theme (performing arts or technology, for example) or are open only to certain children. In some districts, the choice is just among programs within a school building. In any case, find out what options you have, if any. We provide lots of suggestions in Chapter 2 for visiting and evaluating schools.

• *Enroll in classes.* Take advantage of your district's adult and continuing education classes if it has them. Look into the local Y's course offerings or check to see if a community college nearby has courses that interest you. You might find helpful classes on parenting, on child development, on computers, or on something you always wanted to learn, such as French cooking or playing the guitar. By doing this, you show your child again how much you value education.

PARENTS AS TEACHERS

It has become almost a cliché to say that we parents are our children's first teachers. But it's true. Our children learn to talk, to get along with others, to play, to make things, and much, much more only with our guidance and support. Here are just a few examples of ways that we play a teaching role:

• *Provide help at home.* Whether we run to the art store to buy poster board for a special project, arrange for a study partner to come over after school, or quiz our children on math facts, we're teaching. Sometimes we can provide a little tutoring or help them work through difficult homework problems. Both of us have found that this kind of help has made a big difference for our children.

• *Provide opportunities for learning.* Family vacations, weekly treks to the library, outings to the zoo or the museum of natural history—all of these give our children a rich store of information and experience that they bring to school. But even a trip to the grocery store or the veterinarian can become an adventure in learning if we take the time to explain, explore, and encourage questions from our children.

• *Build on your child's interests.* Let's imagine that your child, like one of ours, likes to fish. Family outings or a special day with just Mom or Dad can be built on that interest. But that's only a starting point. How about researching and setting up a fish tank at home? Or visiting the local aquarium? A trip to the library might suggest a specific marine-life interest—sharks, say, or whales. Organizations such as the National Wildlife Federation sponsor activities designed to study and save such animals; your child can adopt a humpback whale, for example. There may be classes or camps offered locally that focus on marine life. With a little research and encouragement on your part, one simple interest can blossom into many areas and become a source of knowledge, competence, and responsibility in which your child can shine.

• *Watch TV together.* Television, too, can provide opportunities for learning. We have found that it works best when we watch a program alongside our children so that we can discuss what's happening, answer questions, and point out details on the spot. Of course, this gives us a better handle on what they're watching, too, so that when they're young, we can turn off inappropriate programs.

• *Balance outside activities.* The "hurried" or overscheduled child is a modern-day phenomenon born of the necessities of busy families and our desire to provide our children with every possible opportunity. Our advice is that more isn't always better. Use common sense when scheduling out-of-school activities. As we discuss later, our children, like us, can get overloaded and cease to function well.

• *Provide a sense of family history and communicate values.* Every family story—whether it's about Grandma's childhood, Dad's stint in the Navy, or Mom's experiences going to night school after working all day—forms an indelible piece of each child's identity. Besides passing on family history, these stories also teach values—what you

and other family members consider important, such as hard
work, a sense of humor, good manners, or patriotism. It
is primarily from us that our children learn social skills,
attitudes toward work and play, and definitions of success,
all of which play a big part in their growth.

• *Be a class parent.* It's really hard to be a class mom or
dad if you don't have free time during the school day.
Usually this hardworking volunteer is present at all class
parties, trips, and other events, having organized the food,
gathered other volunteers, planned games, and done whatever else is needed. The class parent functions almost like
an assistant to the teacher, ensuring that special events run
smoothly and happily. Not everyone can do this, but if you
can, consider it.

• *Attend class trips.* Get a baby-sitter for the baby; take
a day off from work; do whatever you can to go with your
child's class on at least one field trip a year. You'll have
fun with your child and his friends. In addition, you'll have
a chance to observe firsthand how the children get along
with one another and the teacher. Most important, you'll
be able to get involved with what the children are learning
and help your small group get the most out of the trip.

• *Teach a lesson.* A friend of ours was known as "the
picture lady" in her son's elementary school. She visited
several classes a year, slide projector and dozens of slides
and postcards in tow, to share her knowledge and love of
art history. A grandmother we know visited her grand-
daughter's class to talk about her experiences driving an
ambulance during World War II. Do you have a special
hobby or avocation? Do you love your job and want to tell
youngsters about what you do? Do you simply enjoy reading
to children? Any and all of these would be welcomed by
most teachers as enriching their classrooms.

• *Prepare instructional materials.* Perhaps you're a little uncertain about teaching a lesson. Or maybe you can't free up the time during the day. You might be able to share your knowledge anyway, by preparing materials for the teacher to use: slides, handouts, pictures to color, a book to read. Ask the teacher how you can help.

• *Reward your child's hard work.* All the pressure to achieve these days can obscure the importance of effort. A key role for us as parents is to remain equally aware of achievement and effort and to reward both. Sometimes, in fact, persistence and hard work are even more important than the end result, because these are skills that, we hope, become lifelong habits.

PARENTS AS ADVOCATES AND COMMUNICATORS

You'll hear a lot about the role of parents as advocates and communicators throughout this book. This role is especially important because it affects your child so directly. It is also the role you take on when your child is experiencing difficulties of one sort or another. We expand on this in later chapters; what follows is a brief outline of some of the most important ways we can advocate for our children when they need us.

• *Build a relationship with the teacher.* This is absolutely critical, probably the single most important way for us to be involved in our children's educational lives. In Chapter 3, we give lots of tips about how to establish and maintain open lines of communication with the teacher. Only by doing so will you be able to keep up with your child's progress and address any problems that arise.

• *Share your insights about your child.* You know much

more about your child than the teacher ever can. Your
insights, therefore, are invaluable. Don't hesitate to share
them with the teacher, especially when you think more
information will help her understand your child better. A
teacher told us the story of a boy in her class whom she
considered very confident. According to the child's mother,
sometimes this was an act. In a parent-teacher conference,
the mother said that when her son was feeling overwhelmed
he would forget things. The teacher said she used this information to help her determine when the boy needed extra
support.

• *Share information about significant events.* We have
found that most parents don't realize how important it is
to let the teacher know when something at home could be
affecting their child's schoolwork. See Chapter 7 for more
about this.

• *Respond to and give opinions on surveys.* Schools and
school districts frequently send out surveys, asking our
opinions on everything from busing routes to PTA meeting
topics to school activities. Responding to these surveys is
one way of speaking up on behalf of our children.

• *Ask questions.* Another way of making our voices heard
is by asking questions. When you don't understand or don't
like what you hear—be it at a PTA meeting or an open
school night presentation—ask questions. And keep asking
questions.

Let's say you've heard that your district is planning to
put *inclusion* into place—the practice of including special education children in regular classrooms—and you've
also heard that teachers are complaining they're not prepared to deal with these children. Rather than storm a
Board of Education meeting demanding that this not take
place, it would probably be more effective to ask questions.
You might ask which children will be included, how teachers

will be supported, how it will affect other students, how big classes will be, and how the curriculum might be changed. In other words, try to find out the facts about all the things that worry you. By asking these questions, you and other parents not only become part of the discussion, as parents should be, but also hold the school accountable for its practices.

• *Intervene when there's a problem.* All of your hard work, keeping informed and building a relationship with the teacher, really pays off when there's a problem. Then when you step in, your voice is a familiar and respected one. While you won't be able to "fix" all problems, you do want to be heard, so it's important to intervene only when necessary. As a school friend of ours says, "Don't use a cannon when a peashooter will do!" But he also points out that when a cannon is needed, a peashooter is mighty ineffective.

• *Meet with the principal.* It's worth taking the time to get to know the principal. Too often, parents wait until there's a problem to meet with the principal; then just when they need it most, there's no established relationship on which to build. Even if a problem never arises, meeting and talking with the principal gives you another source of information about the school.

• *Help create your child's individual education plan.* If your child has special needs and becomes part of the special education system, you have an important part to play in writing her *individual education plan*—the definition of goals, activities, and special services she'll receive. Your participation in this process will help ensure that all her needs are taken into consideration.

PARENTS AS ACTIVISTS AND DECISION MAKERS

Parents who are activists and decision makers in our schools act on behalf of us and our children, too. They play the important and essential roles that many of us don't choose to or cannot play because of our jobs and other demands on our time or because of our discomfort with the idea of speaking out in public. But there may be ways for you to be an activist or decision maker that fit your time constraints and personality, so don't rule it out. We don't all have to be activists, but we do need to support, inform, and nurture those parents who are. They can't do it alone. Here are a few ideas:

• *Lobby for or against an issue.* There are many opportunities to become involved in a lobbying effort related to the schools. We think of doing this to protect the environment or to get a traffic light installed at a busy corner. The schools, like these other causes, also need our help. Perhaps you'll be called upon to lobby the city government to assign more crossing guards or state or federal legislators to increase funding for schools. Letter-writing campaigns, telephone calls to legislative offices, and position statements read at public hearings are important ways you can help the schools, and they don't necessarily require you to take time off from work.

• *Voice your opinion at school board or parent organization meetings.* Your opinion really does count, so make it known—when the school board is deliberating the budget, when the school has initiated a new attendance policy that doesn't make sense to you, or when you feel a

certain new policy is detrimental to a particular group of parents or children. Plan your remarks and present a rational argument that is likely to convince the schoolpeople.
• *Serve on a principal's advisory committee.* Many principals have advisory committees that meet monthly. If your principal has one, you can volunteer to be a member; if she doesn't, you might want to suggest she start one. Membership on the committee is a good way to get your feet wet and to learn a little bit more about your child's school.

As members of these committees, we've been asked our opinion on everything from the draft of a discipline policy to whether the school should have a coed dance for fifth graders (we voted no because we believed our children were too young to begin dating, and the dance was not held) to what we thought about the new child abuse curriculum. In some cases, the principal asked us to poll a group of parents; other times, all she wanted was our reaction. We learned new things, such as the most recent requirements for graduation, and we shared with the principal things about which we and fellow parents were displeased, such as the science curriculum. We found that a couple of hours once a month was well worth the effort.
• *Become a leader in the parent organization.* The parent organization offers many opportunities to exercise leadership. Parents who are officers in the PTA are typically better informed about what is going on in the school, are more often asked their opinions, and are better known to the school staff. While the position of PTA president is very demanding, not all the other positions are. If you can volunteer to be treasurer or perhaps fund-raising vice-president, you'll be in a better position to steer the organization in the direction you feel it should be headed.
• *Participate in a school governance council.* Many school

districts have now relinquished important decision making on issues such as curriculum, instructional services, and scheduling to school-based governance councils. It is believed in these districts that these decisions should be made as close to the children and staff as possible. While the details vary, most councils include parents in their membership and try to meet at times convenient to both parents and school staff.

Being a member is time-consuming, often frustrating, and not always rewarding. Making decisions as a group is always difficult, and it is especially complicated when parents and teachers are trying to find common ground. Why join, then? Because active parental participation on the councils is critical to their success.

• *Serve on a districtwide committee or task force.* School districts often solicit volunteers from the community to serve on special committees or task forces on issues such as whether to sell a vacant school, full versus half-day kindergarten, and the school budget. Recently, parents in our district joined the staff in exploring ways to save money in the transportation budget. Some of the parents remarked later that it was an eye-opener for them—the issues and the trade-offs discussed were far more complicated than they had imagined.

• *Run for the school board.* After you have been involved in other ways, you might find yourself wanting to be in a position to effect change or put new policies in place. Then you really should consider running for the school board— provided you're ready to devote a *great deal* of extra time (mostly evenings) to this. Our local school board sometimes meets every week.

We believe that the most effective school board members are those who have been involved in many other school activities—PTAs, task forces, or even classroom volunteering—so that they are well informed and have a broad view of school issues.

CONCLUSION

You might be feeling a bit overwhelmed by the dozens of ways we've suggested for you to participate in your child's schooling. Don't. We don't want you to think you have to be a "superparent." There's just no way to do everything we've suggested in this chapter. You'll find a place to start that is comfortable and appropriate for you and your family, just as we did.

It might seem logical to start with the most basic activities listed under "Parents as Supporters" and proceed from there. That will work for some of you. But as we discuss throughout this book, many of you will need to jump right in and become advocates and communicators or even activists and decision makers right away. That might be because your child is experiencing difficulties or because the school isn't living up to your expectations or even just because your district offers you a choice of schools.

You should start with your child, your family, and your school and make your choices based on what's needed and what matters to you. Laurette, who was not working outside the home when her children were young, took an activist role—serving as PTA president in two schools and as head of the districtwide PTA Council. Diane, who has always had a full-time job, focused her attention on activities that directly supported her child. Both roles were appropriate. While our choices were different, our priorities weren't.

We both wanted our children to get the best education possible, just as you do.

FURTHER READING

Linda Albert. *Coping with Kids and School.* New York: E. P. Dutton, 1984.

Melitta J. Cutright. *The National PTA Talks to Parents: How to Get the Best Education for Your Child.* New York: Doubleday, 1989.

Sherry Ferguson and Lawrence E. Mazin. *Parent Power: A Program to Help Your Child Succeed in School.* New York: Clarkson N. Potter, 1989.

Norm Fruchter, Anne Galletta, and J. Lynne White. *New Directions in Parent Involvement.* New York: Academy for Educational Development, 1992.

Haim G. Ginott. *Between Parent and Child.* New York: Macmillan, 1965.

Robin Goldstein. *More Everyday Parenting: The Six- to Nine-Year-Old.* New York: Penguin Books, 1991.

Anne T. Henderson. *The Evidence Continues to Grow: Parent Involvement Improves Student Achievement.* Columbia, MD: National Committee for Citizens in Education, 1987.

————. *Parent Participation—Student Achievement: The Evidence Grows.* Columbia, MD: National Committee for Citizens in Education, 1981.

Marguerite Kelly. *The Mother's Almanac II: Your Child from Six to Twelve.* New York: Doubleday, 1989.

Dorothy Rich. *Megaskills: How Families Help Children Succeed in Schools and Beyond.* Boston: Houghton Mifflin, 1988.

2

WHO'S WHO AND WHAT'S WHAT

A logical place to start participating in your child's schooling is by evaluating his situation. How good is his teacher? How good is the school? These are the first questions we parents want answered. But there are no easy answers. We have to look for ourselves.

This means that we become both learners and activists right away: asking questions; visiting the school and classroom; observing our children, their teachers, and the school; finding out what our options are and then exercising them. To do this well, we must call upon our knowledge of our children and all our parenting and observation skills.

This chapter provides guidelines for evaluating, first, the teacher and classroom and, second, the school as a whole. Our guidelines take the form of questions, not answers. Through them we've tried to give you a framework that will help you focus on considerations we find important. But you'll have to answer your questions in ways that are suitable for you and your child. It has been our experience over and over again that what is appropriate in one case doesn't work in another.

This is more than a fact-finding mission, however. You're evaluating your child's teacher and school in order to determine whether you need to take some action. So we also suggest some possible avenues to take once you have gathered information and reached conclusions. It's crucial to keep in mind that you always have options, and we'll explore some of them with you throughout the book.

To understand the working of the school, we have also found it helpful to understand the larger context. So we close this chapter by briefly visiting the system of which our children's schools are part, introducing the players beyond the school—the district administration, the school board, the state department of education, and the unions.

THE TEACHER AND THE CLASSROOM

What we parents really want to know about teachers is, "How can I recognize a good one?" That is not an easy question to answer. When Patrick, the son of a friend of ours, entered first grade, our friend was dismayed to find out that he had been assigned to Miss Miller. According to other parents, Miss Miller was boring and wouldn't challenge Patrick at all. Our friend decided to wait and see. Much to her surprise, Patrick thrived under Miss Miller's quiet, nurturing style. This unassuming veteran teacher, having uncovered the children's interest in foreign languages, began to teach them French. In retrospect, says our friend, that was probably Patrick's best year in elementary school—in the classroom of a teacher her friends had told her was terrible.

Were her friends wrong? Perhaps not about their children's needs, but they were wrong about Miss Miller and Patrick. Sometimes there is a chemistry at work between a child and a teacher that makes their teaching and learning relationship quite special. Clearly, that was the case here.

Teachers are certified by the state in which they teach. This means they have successfully graduated from an approved course of study, completed a period of student teaching (a kind of apprenticeship), and passed an examination. In New York and many other states, they must then go on to complete a master's degree in order to be permanently certified.

Does certification guarantee that a teacher is good? Of course not: It guarantees no more than a minimum standard of preparation for the job. To answer our questions about good teaching, we parents must rely on our own observations, our common sense, and our knowledge of our children. First, listen to and observe your child at home.

• Does she look forward to going to school?
• Does she feel valued, respected, and cared for by the teacher?
• Does she have chances to show off what she knows and is good at in class?
• Is she learning new skills and knowledge?
• Does she believe that she can do and learn anything, that nothing is too hard for her?

If the answer to all these questions is yes, then chances are your child's teacher is a good one.

But that's not the whole story. You can only get that by visiting your child's classroom to see the teacher in action. In most schools, there's a designated week during the year—officially known as American Education Week and sometimes unofficially as open school week—during which parents are invited to sit in on classes. If you ask, you can visit at other times, too, but don't just drop in unexpectedly. Schedule your visit ahead of time so that the teacher doesn't feel he is being put on the spot.

When you visit, trust your instincts. Look and listen. The following guidelines might help.

GUIDELINES FOR VISITING CLASSROOMS

Children's Reactions and Feelings. Be sure to spend a good part of your time in the classroom watching the children, not the teacher. Their faces, actions, and words will tell you whether or not they feel competent, valued, and challenged. Their interactions with one another and with the teacher will tell you a lot about what it's like to be a member of the class. Here are some specifics you'll want to look for:

• How do the children treat one another? Do they interact with respect? Do they appear to think that everyone has an important contribution to make? Or do they always look to the same few children for answers?

• How do they treat a child who gives a wrong answer? Do they make fun of that child? Or do they appear to consider wrong answers part of the learning process? Do they help one another figure out the right answers?

• Do you see an eagerness to learn expressed in the children's faces, in their responses to questions and assignments, and in their contributions to class discussions?

• Do children take pride in their work? Do they show it to you and to each other? Or is it left lying around, forgotten?

• How do they react when the teacher speaks to them? What can you see in your child's face: affection, pride, humor, fear, dislike, anger? What about other children's faces?

• Do the children appear to enjoy being here? Is there a

sense of fun and productivity in their expressions and behavior?

The Classroom Setup. The way the classroom looks and how it is arranged can tell you a lot about how instruction is carried out and how the children and teacher interact.

• How does the room look overall? Is it cheerful and appealing? Is it set up for children, with furniture, displays, and important information at the right level for them? Is there room to move around, or is it crowded?

• How are the desks arranged? Are they grouped in clusters (telling you that a lot of group work goes on in this classroom)? Or are they all in rows facing forward (telling you that most instruction is teacher-directed)?

• Are there areas around the room where children can work independently? These are called *learning centers*, and usually they accommodate two or three children. Each one is for a specific activity, such as playing with blocks in kindergarten; a listening center in the primary grades, for hearing a tape while following along in the book; a computer corner; a table for conducting experiments with magnetism or electricity. Also look for a quiet reading spot in the room and a private place where a child can be alone or with just the teacher. A classroom organized this way allows for differing styles and paces of learning and enables children to pursue their own interests.

• Look at the bulletin boards. Do you see work displayed by *all* the children? Or only papers with high grades? Do you see several duplicated pages on display, suggesting that the teacher copies assignments from a workbook? Or is there evidence of more creative assignments tailored to this particular class?

• Do you see signs around the room saying "Don't do this"

and "Don't do that," rather than stating rules positively?
• Overall, does the room feel pleasant, organized, and conducive to learning? Is it too neat, hinting that things are on display but not used? Is it too messy, suggesting that things are not used responsibly? Or do you see a comfortable amount of "mess," of work in progress, and mostly clean, organized work areas where children can find what they need?

The Classroom Ambiance. How does it feel to be in this classroom? Is this a place where you would want to spend six hours a day? While the physical appearance of the room contributes to this feeling, the teacher's actions are even more important in helping to create the ambiance in many little and big ways:

• How does the teacher interact with the children? What messages does she give with her face and tone of voice, not with her words? (If you're not sure, look again at the children's reactions.)
• How does she respond to sadness or special news from a child? Is she warm and appropriately attentive? Or does she fail to acknowledge the importance of what the child has told her?
• Does the teacher treat children with respect? Does she answer their questions seriously? Does she acknowledge different ways of learning and different levels of achievement in accepting and respectful ways? How does she respond when a child gives a wrong answer?
• How does the teacher get the children's attention? When they are noisy, does she yell or seem angry or out of control? Or does she have a trick that quiets the children quickly, such as briefly turning off the lights or holding up her hand? This shows you that she has control and that she assumes

that when twenty-odd children are together in one room, there will be noise from time to time.

• How does the teacher handle a misbehaving child? Does she embarrass the child? Is she able to redirect behavior and attention smoothly? What are the consequences of misbehavior? Do the children seem to know about and understand these consequences?

• Overall, is the teacher cheerful? Does she have a sense of humor and fun? Does she seem to enjoy the children?

Instructional Strategies. We saved this for last because most parents think they don't know how to look at a teacher's instructional strategies. Our advice is not to try to be an expert observer. You're probably not one, and you're not concerned about every single thing the teacher does in the classroom anyway. Here are a few things you can observe fairly quickly that will give you much information about the instructional emphasis in this classroom:

• Is the instruction all teacher-directed (the now outdated notion that "teaching is telling, learning is listening"), or is it more varied? (Moving, for example, from teacher-directed instruction with the whole class to working in small groups to working alone or with a partner and then coming back together, with children reporting to one another on what they have learned.)

• Does the teacher write all assignments in at least one prominent place? Does she give children enough time to copy them? Are the assignments clear? Does she also write the goals for the lesson or day and talk about them, so that children understand the purpose of what they're doing?

• Is there evidence of routines in the classroom, of children moving purposefully about, accomplishing particular tasks without being asked?

- Can you see student projects either on display or in process? Are these being done individually, or is the work shared?
- If you see children working in groups, how comfortable do they seem to be with this? Do they work fairly independently, or do they go to the teacher before making decisions?
- Does everyone in the group appear to contribute to the work? Do you observe children playing different roles (leader, recorder, and so forth)?
- Are they productive in their groups or just fooling around? (If they're socializing, don't assume they're fooling around. A benefit of working in small groups is that children can work in a social way, capitalizing on their interest in one another. It's only when the socializing gets out of hand that there's a problem.) How do they draw shy or resistant children into the group work?
- Does the group project or product they're working on seem to be important to them?

WHAT CAN YOU DO?

Before you put your observations together in order to reach a conclusion or make a decision, we have some important caveats.

First, it would be humanly impossible to look at all the things in our guidelines in one visit. Choose one or two areas to focus on, depending on your interests or concerns. Save the rest for another time.

Second, while one visit can give you a lot of information and a good overall impression of the teacher, it's not enough to be the basis of major decisions. For that you need more than one visit or other sources of information.

Finally, not everything on our list is equal to everything else; some things carry more weight.

A friend came to one of us, for example, asking for advice. She had just visited her first-grade daughter's classroom and was distraught to find that very traditional, teacher-directed instruction was obviously the norm. "What should I do?" she asked. "Alex is going to be so bored. She needs to work in groups with other children, not just sit and listen to the teacher all day." A few questions elicited a fuller picture: a warm teacher, happy children, positive relationships, and productive (if traditional) learning activities. While we didn't disagree with our friend, we pointed out all the pluses of this classroom and helped her see that she was overreacting—a common enough occurrence among well-informed parents of primary school children who find less than ideal or less than the most up-to-date instruction. We convinced her to leave Alex where she was, since she was reasonably happy and learning to read.

For another parent, the teacher's rudeness at the school's open house was the first cause for concern. The teacher talked down to parents and harped on the children's faults (as she saw them). The following week, the parent spent an hour in the classroom during open school week. She observed the class working in groups—something our other friend was longing for—but they were making little progress because individual members kept running to the teacher for guidance on what to do next. In addition, the teacher sat at her desk correcting papers instead of moving around and checking on the groups. There was a great deal of laughter and obvious socializing going on. The parent's observations of the lack of structure coupled with the teacher's sarcastic comments to several children caused her to question her child that night. When she asked, "Do you like being in Ms. Andersen's class?" her fifth-grade daughter burst into tears. Only a month into the school year, Althea was already defeated by the confusion and sarcasm.

Meanwhile, parents were talking to one another about the open house rudeness, and many were questioning their children as well. The mother of Althea's friend Sarah was particularly upset. She had gotten to the classroom a few minutes early that night and introduced herself to the teacher. "Sarah's not in my homeroom," said Ms. Andersen. "You belong down the hall in Mr. Jones's room." "I know," said Sarah's mom, "but I wanted to have a chance to introduce myself to you since Sarah has you for language arts." "I don't have time for you now," said Ms. Andersen, turning her back.

But Sarah, much to her mother's surprise, was content in this classroom. "She's not nice all the time, Mom," Sarah reported with equanimity in contrast to Althea's tears, "but she's okay to me."

Sarah's mom therefore did nothing. She did remain diligent, however, watching Sarah's reactions and schoolwork for signs of problems. Althea's parents, on the other hand, got busy. First, they met with Ms. Andersen, explaining that Althea functioned best in situations where expectations were clear and routines well defined. "I have no routines," said Ms. Andersen, breezily dismissing their questions about how her classroom was structured. "And she'll just have to toughen up," she said in response to the parents' characterization of Althea as sensitive to her sarcastic remarks.

Dismayed by these answers, Althea's parents next met with the principal. Stating that Althea needed a more structured environment than Ms. Andersen could provide—an *educational* argument, not one based on personalities— they convinced the principal to move her to another class.

THE SCHOOL: WHAT YOU SEE IS WHAT YOU GET—OR IS IT?

The school plays critically important roles in the lives of our children. It will mold their attitudes about themselves, about education, and about their friends and the world around them. It is also the place where much of their character will be developed, their study and learning habits formed, and their goals for the future shaped.

We hope that our guidelines for evaluating schools will change the way you think about every school you enter from now on. Maybe you have a child starting school for the first time, or perhaps you are thinking of moving to a new school zone or a new district, or maybe you are among the fortunate parents who can choose their children's elementary schools. Whatever the reason, we encourage you to visit the school and assess what you see for yourself—and not make your decision based on what others say.

As you walk around the school, think about its climate. By this we mean the temperament of the building, not its temperature. Our questions are designed to help you decide what its ambiance, tone, or culture is. We leave it up to you to decide whether that matches what you want for your child.

GUIDELINES FOR VISITING THE SCHOOL

We want to warn you, first, that we will not be giving you a template for a perfect school. Rather, we will point out things for you to look for and think about. At the end, we'll show you what one parent did with her observations of schools and her knowledge of her child.

The Entrance. The main entrance of the building provides
your first impression of the school, and we all know that
first impressions can be very telling.

- Is the front entrance clearly marked so that you know
which door to enter? Is it inviting? Or is the only sign you
see the one we hate: "Visitors report immediately to the
office"?
- Once you're in the building, what greets you? Is there a
friendly welcoming sign? Do you see student work immediately? Is there a sense that children "live" here?

The Office. The office is the hub of every school, a place
exploding with teachers, children, telephones, and stacks
of paperwork. At the center is the school secretary. She is
supposed to perform efficiently despite the fact that her
work is interrupted dozens of times an hour because a child
lost a sweater, another has a tooth that just came out, a
teacher can't find his supply of weekly magazines for the
class, and the phone is ringing off the hook. The secretary
will save you when you forget to tell your daughter that
your friend will be picking her up instead of you, and she'll
help you when you need to arrange a meeting with a teacher
or the principal. Be sure to learn the secretary's name, and
at the end of the year when you are writing thank-you notes,
include her on your list.

Now look for these clues to the school's "personality":

- Are there signs clearly directing you to the main office?
- Is the office neat and orderly? Friendly?
- What happens when you enter the office? Are you greeted
warmly and immediately by the school secretary, or do you
have to wait a few minutes or more before she helps you?
- If you have an appointment, are you met on time or are

you kept waiting? If you have to wait, are you given an apology and explanation?

• How are the children treated when they come into the office? Are they welcomed and greeted by name? Are they made to wait before getting any attention?

• Why are the children in the office? Are they being punished? Or are they showing off a project well done?

The Halls. As you walk around the building, you'll get an overall sense of its tone.

• Is the school neat and clean? Are the halls well lighted? Do you see signs of peeling paint or leaky water faucets?

• Are the hallways full of children's artwork, displays, and schoolwork? Or are they decorated by the teachers with materials purchased from the local teacher's store? Are the displays at the children's eye level?

• Have you ever seen a display of children's art in which each piece of work looks exactly like the others? Do you see that here, showing that art instruction is heavily teacher-directed? Or is each piece of art unique?

• If there are pictures, do they mirror the student population? For example, if the school is one-third white, one-third African American, and one-third Latino, then it's just not acceptable to see pictures of only white children in the halls.

• Are the displays in good shape? Or are they faded, torn, and falling off the walls? The message children get from unkempt displays is that their work is not valued.

"Special" Rooms. These are the rooms where instruction in special subjects takes place—the art and music rooms, the gym, and the auditorium. Some districts shortchange students by putting very little money aside for these "spe-

cials." You can judge what your district's priorities are by taking a look around the rooms.

• Are the rooms in good repair? Are they set up attractively; that is, do you think your child will have a good time in the room?
• Is the art room well stocked? Does it have drawing tables at the right height for the students using them? Does it seem bright and full of life?
• Does the music room have a piano that's not a relic? Does it have other instruments, and are they in good shape?
• How about the gym? Are the floors shiny and well cared for? Or are they warped and dull? What is the condition of the other equipment? (Floor mats with the stuffing spilling out tells us that physical education is a low priority in the school.) Does there seem to be enough equipment for a typical class to use?
• Is the auditorium designed only for large groups of people sitting passively and watching performers on the stage? We have found such auditoriums to be used infrequently in schools. When you are on your tour, ask how the room is used. We've seen auditoriums that were extremely interactive. They were set up with movable side walls to make the room smaller and more conducive to small group use. We've also seen one set up like an amphitheater, with no seats at all, just carpeted steps; it was designed for active use by students in both small and large groups.

The Playground. This place is very important to our children. It deserves careful scrutiny.

• Is the playground in good repair? Is it safe? Are little bodies exposed to rusty metal parts or splintered wood? Is

the ground cover cement or some other, softer surface that
would cushion a child's fall?
• Does the playground contain equipment developmentally
suited to the varied ages of the children in the school? Is
the equipment too big or too small? Is there enough space
for children to play large group games such as jump rope,
tag, or kickball?
• Don't look only at the equipment; look also at the people
supervising the children. Are they having a good time with
the children, or are they clustered together talking to one
another? Are their eyes circling their patrol area, antici-
pating problems or occasions for intervention? When they
speak to children, are they polite?
• Are the children having fun? Are they playing together
nicely? Or does it appear that older kids are bullying the
younger ones—with no intervention from the playground
supervisors?

The Principal. As the CEO of the school, the principal sets
the tone and standards for the building, so spending some
time with her is worthwhile. It's her job to make on-the-
spot decisions dealing with everything from where to hold
lunch recess—indoors or outdoors—to whether or not to
recommend a teacher for tenure.

It's not easy to become a principal. In New York, the
requirements include a stint as a classroom teacher, a special course of study, an internship, and state certification.
What makes the difference between a good principal and a
mediocre one, however, is not educational credentials. It
is *leadership*. The principal's leadership style will tell you
a lot about the climate of the school she heads. Consider
the following.

- How does the principal interact with children? Is she respectful? Is the interaction natural, or does it appear to be put on for you? Are children treated with warmth, and are they greeted by name?
- What does she do when she sees a misbehaving child? Does she intervene effectively? How does the child react?
- How does the principal interact with the staff? Is it respectful? Does there seem to be a positive give-and-take? Does the principal introduce you, and if so, how are you greeted by the staff?
- Which classrooms and teachers does she take you to visit? You can tell a lot about her educational values based on this. For example, if a principal takes you only into traditional classrooms, with desks in rows facing forward and only *A* papers on display, you might conclude that she believes in that educational approach. Ask her. As we've already indicated, we prefer a different kind of classroom!
- How does the principal view parent participation? Is she satisfied with the role of parents as fund-raisers? Or does she encourage a broader range of roles? You'll have to ask some questions about this, such as: "Do you have an advisory group that includes parents?" "Are parents included when you have discussions about changing the curriculum or textbooks?" How interested is she to hear your insights about your child?
- How much time does she spend with you? Does she welcome your questions? Do you feel rushed?

Specialists. Most schools employ a variety of specialists—including reading teachers, teachers of the gifted, and speech therapists—to help students with special needs. As you walk around the school, look for and ask about these special programs.

• Ask what programs are available. Who teaches them? What qualifications do these specialists have?

• Where do these programs meet? Do these specialists have their own rooms? Where are these rooms located? Are they well equipped with books and other materials? Are they cheerful, pleasant places for learning? How many children can they accommodate at once?

• To whom are these services available? Sometimes specialists are funded by state or federal grants to help only a particular group of children. Other times, a child must demonstrate a specific need or receive a specific score on certain exams to be eligible. Find out how it works in your school.

• Ask whether specialists take children out of class or work side by side with teachers in the classroom or, best of all, do some of both. For many years so-called pull-out programs were the rage because of the focused individual attention they could provide. The disadvantage was the fragmentation of the children's learning. Nowadays, specialists prefer to work in the classroom whenever possible so that children will not miss their regular work or be singled out as "different."

• Ask whether the school has a full-time nurse. If she works part-time, who handles medical problems when she's not there? This question will be particularly important to you if your child suffers from asthma or another chronic medical condition.

WHAT CAN YOU DO?

What happens when you do what we suggest? You visit the school, you sit in on a classroom, and you now have several

pages of notes. What should you do with all this? Let's
follow a hypothetical scenario.

A CASE STUDY

Janet Jones was a single parent who commuted daily to the
city to her job as art director in an advertising agency.
Janet wanted to move, and she looked at condominiums in
two of her district's three school zones. In order to decide
where to live, Janet set out to investigate the elementary
school in each zone for her eight-year-old son Matthew. She
thought about the things he liked to do: He was artistic like
his mom, an average student, and somewhat shy and sensitive. They were living in a small community, and the
elementary school he currently attended had only 250
children.

The principal at School A greeted Janet promptly and
immediately took her on a tour of the school. The building
was old and in desperate need of a paint job in some areas.
The playground, though safe, was somewhat sparsely
equipped compared with her son's current school.

During the tour, Janet noticed that the principal greeted
most children by their first names, and Janet sensed their
mutual respect and affection. She was pleased to learn that
all children had art daily. She observed the art displayed
in the hallways and found it very creative, although it appeared that the art budget wasn't huge.

Janet explained that Matthew had some problems with
math due to a slight learning disability. She told the principal she was concerned that his problem, though slight,
would be overlooked in such a large school (over five
hundred students). The principal asked Janet a few questions about Matthew and explained the school's mentoring
system. He told her that her child's mentor—an adult,

not necessarily his teacher—would be in touch with her as soon as she registered to get information from her and her son. This mentor would be responsible for tailoring Matthew's school program to meet his educational, emotional, and social needs and for monitoring his progress.

Janet's experience in School B was in some ways very similar, yet in other ways quite different. The school building was also old but was better maintained. Its new playground put the first one to shame.

Janet was greeted by a very warm principal who apologized for keeping her waiting. The principal explained that she was delayed because she was meeting with a group of youngsters interested in starting a student council. She said they were so enthusiastic, she hated to end the discussion.

Janet noticed that hallway displays were not as colorful and artistic as those in School A, and she asked the principal if art was offered daily. The principal explained that art was taught by the classroom teacher, not by a specialist. She said the faculty had "traded in" the art teacher for a computer specialist when the former retired.

In response to Janet's questions, the principal described how Matthew would be evaluated in math and how the classroom teacher would provide him with assistance, if he needed it, during recess time. She also said the teacher would meet with Janet to discuss activities that Janet could do each evening with her son to strengthen his math skills. The principal said the teachers relied on the parents to work with the children at home because they were too busy during the day to provide individualized instruction. The school had prepared special at-home kits for just such cases.

After the visits, Janet reflected on her observations and on her conversations with both principals. She concluded that either school would be good enough for her son, but for a number of reasons she felt that School A would be better for Matthew. Janet was worried that she wasn't qualified and didn't have the time to work with Matthew each evening—something that seemed to be part of the philosophy of School B. Evenings were special times for this mother and child. After a fast dinner, Matthew did his homework while she read the local paper. Then they usually did an art project together before his bath and then his bedtime story. She didn't want to change the routine that was working well for them, and she didn't like the idea that shy Matthew would be taken away from recess to do schoolwork. She believed that he needed as much socializing as possible.

In addition, Janet was concerned about the lack of imagination and creativity she had observed in the artwork in the hallways and classrooms of School B. This was a serious issue for her; the sparse playground equipment was not. Janet also liked the fact that at School A one person would get to know Matthew well and would be responsible for his overall progress.

Janet was not an educator, but just a few hours of observation and questioning gave her enough information to make a decision. She knew her son and balanced his needs against what she found in both schools.

WHAT IF?

Most of us don't have a choice of schools as Janet did. Sometimes we're lucky to get just the right match. Most of the time, however, we get a school that's less than perfect but still "good enough" for our children. Once in a while —rarely, thank goodness—we get one that's not even that. Let's see what Janet's story might have been if she had bought her home before visiting the schools and had been assigned to School B or School C.

School B. In the case of School B, Janet probably would have felt that she had found a school that was good enough for Matthew. By "good enough," in this case, we mean a school headed by a warm and caring principal who listened to children's ideas; a school that valued parents so much, it entrusted some of the instruction to them; a school that understood the power of technology. Okay, it didn't have an art teacher, and it required Janet to be involved in Matthew's instruction at home. Janet would have had to make some adjustments.

"Good enough" almost always means that we parents have some work to do. Some relatively simple strategies would have worked for Janet, and they can work for you if you find yourself in this situation.

• *Communicate with schoolpeople.* Janet could have let each of Matthew's teachers know about his learning problem and also about his artistic ability—a simple letter introducing herself and Matthew would have done the trick. She could have explained that she was willing to help her son at home but had no experience as a teacher and little time as a single parent.

• *Provide extra support at home.* Janet might have had to give up her newspaper at night and spend more time supervising Matthew's homework. She probably would also have had to help him with some extra practice activities in the evening.

• *Watch more carefully at home.* Remaining vigilant was one of the most important things Janet could have done for Matthew: asking him questions, checking his homework and test papers, observing his behavior and comments about school, and talking with other parents as she got to know them.

• *Volunteer in school to supplement what is inadequate.* Perhaps Janet could have offered to lead art activities in the class or even after school if her company was willing to give her the time off.

• *Provide outside activities to enrich and support your child's education.* Janet could also have enrolled Matthew in a Saturday art class at the local YMCA or spent some extra time with him on weekends.

• *Organize other parents.* Janet could have attended PTA meetings and talked to other parents to see if they shared her concern that there was no art teacher. If they did, Janet could have set up an appointment with the principal to talk about reinstating a formal art program.

School C. Now it could have been much worse. Suppose the school Janet was assigned to—let's call it School C— had nothing at all going for it. What could Janet have done when her observations and her instincts told her that it was all wrong for Matthew? (This doesn't happen often and probably won't happen to you, but many parents worry about it, so let's explore this possibility a little further.)

We would have recommended, first, that Janet think about and try to define what bothered her about the school. Was it the school's ambiance, the attitude of the principal and staff toward one another and the students, the facility, the course offerings, the lack of specific specialized services? Or was it that she felt a lack of respect for her as a parent? Once she defined her misgivings, Janet could have taken a couple of avenues to acquire more information:

• Janet could have called the school and asked for the names and telephone numbers of several parents. (The school should have had no problem giving Janet the names of PTA officers; they're usually published in school directories.) Janet could have made a few calls and asked the parents open-ended questions about her concerns. For example, if she felt the principal was rude to her, as shown by keeping her waiting, she could have asked if this was typical treatment of parents.

• She could also have telephoned the principal to ask for clarification. Because her son needed help with math, Janet might have been concerned that the school didn't seem to have resources to help Matthew in that area. This is a concern the principal should have been able to address.

Janet could also have looked into placement in another school in the district. Someone in the superintendent's office could have told her how to go about this. She (and any parent asking for an out-of-zone placement) would have needed to plead her case well. How she framed her argument would have been crucial. It's doubtful that the district would have granted her request if, for example, it was based on personality or feelings—affective reasons. She would have had more luck if she framed her argument in terms of Matthew's educational needs, just as Althea's parents did in our earlier example.

In this case, Janet might have argued that the support Matthew needed in math was available at School A and not at School C. She could also have pointed out that at School B, Matthew would have had to give up recess in order to receive extra help.

Janet's story is only slightly different from the case where parents are unhappy with the school their children are already attending and request a transfer. An additional important consideration in that case is how a child feels

about changing schools. If you're considering this, you need
to know your child and weigh the advantages and disad-
vantages of moving against those of staying.

If Janet's placement request was denied or if no other
schools were available, then her work would have been cut
out for her. She would have had to use the same strategies
we suggested for School B but remain even more vigilant.
She would have had to be on top of everything and might
even have had to reorder her priorities, possibly using some
of her vacation days, to spend more time in school meeting
with the principal or Matthew's teacher or maybe volunteering in his class. And she would definitely have had to
forgo reading the newspaper at night in order to spend time
reviewing Matthew's work, helping him with math, or writing to the teacher.

We've used Janet Jones's story to illustrate the fact that
we parents always have options; we are not powerless.
Sometimes we can choose a school; sometimes we can take
action to change placement in a school or classroom; sometimes we can offer our own time and expertise to improve
our children's experiences; sometimes we can add to these
experiences outside of school; and sometimes we can just
be present as support for our children. It's important for
us to be *active*, to be *informed*, and to be *open-minded*
when looking at our options so that we can do what's best
for our children.

THE SCHOOL'S RESPONSIBILITIES TO PARENTS

Remember, it's not entirely up to you. While it is up to you to get involved in ways that will help your child, it is up to the school to make this possible. Some of the school's responsibilities include the following:

• Expecting and, when necessary, training teachers to work with you.
• Consulting regularly with you about how the schools can work better with you.
• Providing a range of opportunities for you to become informed and involved.
• Giving you support, including training if needed, so that you can understand the school's programs and be able to help your child at home.
• Remaining accountable to you—reporting to you on your child's progress, including scheduling parent-teacher conferences at mutually convenient times.
• Responding in a timely manner to your concerns.
• Giving you a true feeling of partnership in your child's schooling.

THE SYSTEM

It's been our experience that most parents don't understand the whole system of education into which their children's schools fit. Why does that matter? Because knowledge is power, and, as we've already said, we're more effective advocates when our stance is an informed one. Parents we know who have organized a group for some particular purpose—such as supporting (or opposing) a principal for tenure or influencing the school budget—have also been more successful and have been treated with more respect when they understood the way the larger system works.

THE DISTRICT

The school your child attends is part of a district that includes the elementary, middle (or junior high), and high schools in your town or region. In charge of running the district, making decisions, and supervising all employees is the superintendent. She is not someone you are likely to meet in the course of your normal school routines, but you can see her in action at school board meetings and at other district meetings. It's rare that you would need to meet with her, but you might want to if you have a district issue to raise—if your school district doesn't offer instrumental music, for example, and you want to make an argument for adding it to the district's programs. You might also want to consult her if you have a problem or issue that remains unresolved after you've exhausted the problem-solving routes we've suggested here.

Most superintendents call upon the advice and help of a group of assistant superintendents in charge of such areas as curriculum and instruction, business, personnel, pupil support services, and communications and public information; this group is sometimes referred to as the *cabinet*. Additional professionals with expertise in all these areas usually work in the district or central office, too.

THE SCHOOL BOARD

The superintendent is not autonomous; she answers to the local school board. This group, which varies in size from town to town, is usually elected by school district residents.

Most of the time the members serve without pay. They set policy for the school district; they do not administer the schools or supervise employees. They might debate issues such as whether the middle-level schools should be grades six to eight or seven to nine, for example, and whether or not the district should have a full-day kindergarten. But once they have decided, the professional staff organizes, designs, and implements the program.

Most school boards meet at least monthly, and by law all meetings are open to the public except when matters of personnel or real estate are being discussed. We urge you to attend some meetings. You'll get invaluable insight into important issues, and you can find out how your board members make decisions and what stands they take. Usually, meetings are conducted in a rather formal manner, and members of the public can speak or ask questions only at designated times. But at those times you can say what you think, and you should. Many parents tell us that the first time they attended a board meeting they were intimidated by the formality; we were, too. But after a while, you'll realize, as we did, that the board is made up of people just like you and your neighbors.

If you can't go to meetings every month, a good way to keep track of your school board is through the local newspaper. Here you should be able to find out about the controversies and important issues before the board. If your board is in the newspaper too often, however, this may be a sign of instability. Try to read between the lines: Are members squabbling constantly? Are they fighting with the superintendent? Are they concerned about the children or their own power? You might also be able to stay informed about the board through a district newsletter if there is one. Find out who mails it out, and make sure your name is on the list.

The school budget is a very important function of the school board. In most towns, citizens vote on the budget, which determines their school taxes. In a few localities, the school board decides the budget by itself. Either way, it's a good idea to attend a meeting on the budget to familiarize yourself with the issues, the proposed increases or cuts, and the impact these will have on your child. By attending these meetings you'll see the budgetary tug of war for yourself: how to balance children's real needs against the constraints of funding levels. If there's an issue you feel passionately about, you might want to get together with other like-minded parents to make your case.

THE STATE DEPARTMENT OF EDUCATION

Even the school board is not autonomous. In each state a department of education, headed by a commissioner or superintendent and guided by a board of education, sets policies, guidelines, and minimum standards to which every school district must adhere. It sets the minimum number of days students must attend school each year, for example, and makes decisions concerning standardized testing. A local school board cannot eliminate such testing, therefore, if it is required by the state. Sometimes there are procedures for obtaining waivers or exemptions from certain requirements if the district can demonstrate that it is meeting the state's minimum standards in another way.

States also provide a fairly substantial amount of funding to each school district. While some of this is distributed on the basis of competitive grants, most is issued according to a formula that takes into account the relative wealth of each district as well as the needs of students. There's a great deal of debate about whether these formulas are fair.

Some activists believe that state monies should be used to
equalize per-student spending across districts so that students in poorer areas, especially inner cities, aren't pe-
nalized by where they live. New Jersey is trying to put this
into effect. This is very controversial because parents and
educators in wealthier districts don't want to lose state
funds, which would force them to cut back their programs.
Proponents of this policy believe that creating equity in
educational funding is a critically important state responsibility.

THE UNIONS

Some parents are surprised to discover how much influence
the unions, particularly those representing teachers, have
on their children's schooling. This influence is exerted primarily through the contract, which is renegotiated every
few years. If your district is unionized—and not all are—
it probably negotiates with at least a teachers' and an administrators' union. There might also be a civil service
union representing some out-of-classroom personnel.

Each contract is a legal document between a particular
union and the school board. In addition to spelling out
salaries, benefits, and pensions, the contract often deals
with educational matters in the district as well. It almost
always spells out the hours a teacher can be required to
work, usually restricting evening hours to a certain number
per year; sometimes it sets limits on class sizes; often it
determines out-of-classroom assignments, such as lunch
duty. So if a district wants to offer more evening activities
for parents, say, it may find that the contract makes it
difficult if not impossible to do so.

FURTHER READING

Ernest Boyer. *High School: A Report on Secondary Education in America.* New York: Harper Colophon Books, 1983.

John T. Goodlad. *A Place Called School: Prospects for the Future.* New York: McGraw-Hill, 1984.

Making Sense of School Budgets: A Citizen's Guide to Local Public Education Spending. Washington, DC: U.S. Department of Education, 1989.

David Schimmel and Louis Fischer. *Parents, Schools, and the Law.* Columbia, MD: National Committee for Citizens in Education, 1987.

Daniel Seymour and Terry Seymour. *America's Best Classrooms: How Award-Winning Teachers Are Shaping Our Children's Future.* Princeton, NJ: Peterson's Guides, 1992.

Theodore R. Sizer. *Horace's School: Redesigning the American High School.* New York: Houghton Mifflin, 1992.

3

GETTING IN TOUCH AND STAYING IN TOUCH

The role of advocate and communicator is essential to our children's success in school. That's because opening up the lines of communication with our children's teachers—and keeping them open—enables us to identify problems our children might be having, to collaborate in solving them, and sometimes to prevent them from becoming problems in the first place. By building a productive relationship with the teacher, we become true partners in our children's educational lives. That may sound corny, but it's true.

Like any human relationship, our partnership with the teacher takes thought and work, by us and by the teacher. In this chapter, we share some basic principles of communication—simple ideas that come from our own experiences and those of our friends over the years. We also take you through a couple of sample parent-teacher conferences in order to illustrate lessons about preparing for, participating in, and following up on these meetings. Throughout, we remind you that effective communication depends as much on listening as it does on talking. A teacher

friend of ours begins every conference with parents by saying, "Tell me about your child." And then she listens. She
learns new things every time, she says, from what parents
tell her.

We parents can learn just as much if we're willing to
listen to what teachers have to tell us about our children.
A friend of ours gained new perspectives on her son at a
middle school parent-teacher conference. The teacher, who
had carefully observed Carl, told our friend how impressed
she was by his leadership qualities. This was a surprise to
Carl's mom, who saw her son as well liked by his peers but
had never thought of him as a leader. The teacher was
concerned because Carl tended to use his abilities to or-
chestrate naughty or silly behavior by his classmates. Together, the teacher and our friend decided to encourage
Carl to run for student government. He did—and won a
seat—thanks to the insights of an observant teacher.

BASIC PRINCIPLES

LISTENING TO OUR CHILDREN

About a month or six weeks into his kindergarten year, the
son of a friend came home with stories about being punished
by having to sit on a chair. Our friend listened, asked
questions, tried to sort out what was actually happening
and why, but without success. She told us that she had
visions of Sean sitting in the corner, a dunce hat on his
head. So she called the teacher right away and made an
appointment.

We've learned the hard way to trust our instincts. When
we think there's a problem, we get in touch with our children's teachers immediately. We don't believe in waiting to

see if the problem will go away or if the teacher will contact us. In most cases, the teachers are glad to hear from us, to know that we are concerned, and to have a chance to work with us to help our children.

And Sean did have a problem. As we'll show, it wasn't quite the problem he presented, nor was it what his mother imagined. But if your child believes there's a problem, then something is probably wrong. Remember, though, that a five-year-old (or even a thirteen-year-old) doesn't see the big picture. Don't accept your child's version of what happened as gospel, but do something about it, as Sean's mom did, before it becomes a bigger problem for your child.

LISTENING TO THE TEACHER

Our friend told us she showed up for her appointment with sweaty palms. She began the conference as we recommend, by asking the teacher to clarify what had happened. She found out that Sean was indeed being singled out. During circle time, when all the children gathered on the floor, he couldn't stop chatting. Putting him on a chair, in the group but a little above the other children, seemed to help him focus, the teacher had found.

Sean's mother approached the teacher with an open mind. Convinced there was a problem, she solicited and listened to the teacher's perceptions of her son, and it turned out that her worst visions were not a reality: Sean was not being punished, and he wasn't sitting in the corner wearing a dunce cap. In fact, the teacher was struggling to find a way to help him learn self-control.

Whenever our children are experiencing difficulties in school, we parents feel a lot of pain. That's natural. However, we have to learn not to react to that pain by jumping to conclusions or lashing out at the teacher or at our children. We must not assume that our children are right or, even worse, wrong. It's rarely that simple.

SHARING INFORMATION

In our friend's case, she had important information to share with the teacher, too—information she didn't even realize was important. She casually mentioned that the family had just moved and, as a result, Sean didn't know a single child in the school. What appeared to be chatting with friends was actually making friends, a subtle but big distinction to the teacher. "I'll deal with it differently from now on," she assured our friend. "And I have some suggestions on how you can help Sean, too." Together they worked on resolving the problem without putting Sean on a chair anymore.

In order to deal appropriately with our children, teachers need to know basic facts. If his teacher had been aware in September that Sean did not know anyone in the class, she probably would have handled his chattiness differently. Sometimes what appears minor to us as adults takes on greater importance to our children. So when in doubt, tell the teacher. Of course, major changes or events in our families' or children's lives—such as moving, divorce, death, or illness—should always be shared with the teacher because they will undoubtedly be reflected in our children's behavior in school.

AN EXCEPTION

Having declared that you should contact the teacher right away when you think there's a problem, we now want to contradict ourselves. Sometimes the best thing to do is not to talk with the teacher. Here's what we mean.

My son Pete's third-grade teacher insisted on calling him
Red. (He has red hair.) He hated the nickname. One day
he came home and said to me, "Mom, I want you to have
Mrs. Zabriskie fired because she calls me Red."

I told him that wasn't appropriate and suggested instead
that he go to Mrs. Zabriskie quietly before class and ask
her not to call him Red anymore, explaining that he didn't
like the name. He was a little nervous, but I told him that
I thought he was grownup enough to handle this himself.

He did, the very next morning. Unfortunately, Mrs. Za-
briskie then embarrassed him by praising him to the class.
"Most kids would have gone home and said, 'Mom, I want
Mrs. Zabriskie fired,' " she said, much to Pete's surprise.

But she didn't call him Red anymore.

This mother helped her son deal with a problem himself.
She believed that he was ready, that the problem did not
require her intervention, and that the teacher would respond to the boy. She was right. Despite the teacher's
clumsy handling of the situation, the problem was resolved.

The most important thing Pete learned was that he could
effect change himself. Sometimes the best way for us to help
our children is by teaching them to help themselves. The
hard part is figuring out when they're ready for this. We
can't tell you when your child is ready to jump in and fend
for himself. No one can; you'll have to gauge that for yourself. Observe his reaction to your suggestion. Look at what
his friends are doing: Are some of them a little more independent than he is? Take into consideration how he reacts
to new situations: Does he tend to be timid at first, for
example? You might have to prod him a little, as our friend
did. The worst that will happen if he's not ready or can't
handle the problem is that you'll have to follow up yourself.
It's worth the risk.

GETTING IN TOUCH

The way we approach teachers, principals, guidance counselors, or other school employees gives them a message. We need to let them know that we respect their time, skills, and knowledge of our children, but we also need to let them know that we expect their respect in return and their prompt attention to our concerns. Finding the right balance isn't any easier with schoolpeople than with anyone else, but it's crucial. Here are a couple of tips that we have found can help.

Find out how the school wants you to make appointments. Most school handbooks spell this out. If not or if there isn't a handbook, call the school office and ask the secretary. Usually a note to the teacher or a message left with the secretary will work. Some principals we've worked with have call-in hours before school from 7:30 to 8:00 a.m. when you can discuss issues or make appointments. Whether you write or call, give your name, the nature of your request, the times you're available to meet, and your phone number. If you don't hear anything in a day or two, try again.

Don't approach people on the run. If you see the principal in the hall or your child's teacher at a school concert, don't give in to the temptation to talk to him on the spot about what's bothering you. This is the pet peeve of a principal friend of ours: "When parents see me, they always want to talk about their children right then and there. Holiday concert night is a relaxed, social time for them but not for me. I'm working! I'm there to direct traffic and to say 'Hello. How are you?' but not to discuss which reading groups their children should be in."

STAYING IN TOUCH

As our children get older, they tend to share less and less information with us about school, friends, and other things that are important to them. This means it's up to us to stay current with their progress and work in school, and this takes some intentional effort. In addition to reviewing their homework, a few ideas that have worked for us and other parents we know include the following:

Talk about school at home. We all need to have some regular family time for catching up and talking things over. This might be right after school if you're home then; it might be over dinner if you're able to eat together regularly; it might be at bedtime or even on Sunday mornings. Whenever it is, this is the time for conversation about school, among other things. A few casual questions between mouthfuls of pasta may elicit a wealth of information. Don't ask questions about how your child did on the spelling or history test, although you will want to find that out, too, but ask more interesting ones: "Are you still learning about the rain forest? Tell me about it: I don't know a lot about that." Often, your child will do that eagerly when given the opportunity to be the expert. Let him teach you about the rain forest, and as he describes classroom activities, you'll learn a lot about how he's doing in school.

Contact the teacher every so often. Write a note to the teacher about something positive: a funny story or a touching comment about her from your child, an observation you've made about your child's progress. Or write just to say you think things are going well and ask if she agrees. Send in a homemade valentine or a batch of healthy snacks for the class. This kind of communication gives the message that you're "with her," that you see her as a partner, and that you appreciate her. You'll also earn goodwill for yourself and your child; then when there's a problem, the teacher will contact you right away and assume that you'll help. That in itself helps your child.

KEEPING TRACK

We've found it useful to keep a file of school-related matters, including copies of formal records such as medical forms, report cards, and school reports. In addition, you should probably keep records of all communications from and to the school and teacher: phone calls, conferences, conversations, and letters (from you or from the teacher). Jot down some notes on a calendar or log just a few details. You may never need to refer to these records, but if a problem develops later or if memory fails, you'll be very happy to have your notes.

THE PARENT-TEACHER CONFERENCE

The most traditional example of direct personal communication between us and our children's teachers is the parent-teacher conference. Usually, these are scheduled for all parents a month or so after school begins so that parents and teachers can get to know each other and the students better. Sometimes conferences are scheduled again in the spring after standardized test results are in. Once in a while, teachers ask to meet with parents for specific reasons at other times. We parents can request conferences, too—and we should!—at any time we need to meet face-to-face with the teacher.

There can be many reasons for such a request: if a child

who always loved school suddenly says she hates it, if a child is struggling for hours every night with homework, if the home situation has changed because of serious illness or divorce, or if you don't understand your child's placement in a particular reading group.

Every issue doesn't require a conference, however. A short note or phone call to the teacher can resolve many small issues, such as clarifying which days your son should bring his trumpet to school or whether it's okay to send in cupcakes on his birthday. But more difficult problems, such as persistent teasing by a classmate or nightly difficulties with math homework, might require a face-to-face meeting. Use your judgment to decide what is called for.

One year, for example, the preadolescent daughter of a friend came home nearly every week terribly hurt by something the teacher had said or done. Our friend talked it over with her daughter each time, only to realize that the hurt came more from the girl's ultrasensitive age and stage than from the teacher's actions. Her job was not to call the teacher but rather to help her daughter see that the teacher hadn't meant to hurt her.

But if you decide a conference is needed, don't ever hesitate to request one.

Daytime conferences are most common, but some districts schedule them in the evening, too. Since we both work, we often meet with teachers very early in the morning, at 7:45 or 8:00. When a teacher schedules an appointment for you that is impossible to keep, send her a note with a list of alternative times—perhaps early in the morning would be good for you, too, or at the end of the school day. If you cannot negotiate a mutually agreeable time with the teacher, you might be able to arrange for a telephone conference. We've heard of schools doing that regularly for working parents.

Both parents and teachers come to these conferences with personal histories, and not all of these are positive. Sometimes past experiences can cause conferences to get off to a bad start.

Unfortunately, most teachers do not receive training in how to conduct a meeting with parents or on the importance of developing a partnership with them. Frequently, they are influenced by the experiences of their peers, as this young faculty member was:

> I was dreading my conference with Ms. Lawrence because of the story a colleague told in the teacher's lounge. The year before, that colleague said he had had a very confrontational conference with her. In fact, it had required a follow-up conference, with the principal acting as mediator.
>
> I was sick at the thought that this might happen to me. As a new teacher, I didn't feel confident about handling a difficult parent.
>
> All my agonizing was for nothing. I found Ms. Lawrence to be very receptive to what I had to say and very forthcoming about her son's strong and weak points.

This young teacher learned an important lesson: Each situation and set of players is unique. It was not helpful for the teacher to prejudge Ms. Lawrence, just as it doesn't help for us to prejudge a teacher because one child's experience in the class was not great.

For more seasoned teachers, occasional bad experiences with parents or perhaps some defensiveness about their teaching can cause them to view conferences with trepidation.

Some parents may also have had bad experiences with a teacher or school or might feel inadequate or defensive;

what teachers have to say about their children may be heard as criticisms of their parenting skills.

I felt so awful when my son's teacher told me he exhibited total lack of control in the classroom. Charles is the youngest of five children, all under ten, and our household is extremely chaotic. I felt that she was telling me that I had done a bad job with my large family.

Knowing that anxiety and inexperience can exist on both sides, parents and teachers must do whatever they can to create positive conferences. Yet despite everyone's best intentions, this doesn't always happen. One teacher we know tells us he always worries about—and spends extra time preparing for—conferences with parents when their children are having problems:

I knew it was going to be difficult talking to Mr. Peters about his son's problems in math. I had been trying on my own for weeks to give Tom extra help, but he wasn't making enough progress. I needed his parents' help, too.

In anticipation of our meeting, I made some notes about Tom's difficulties and what I had been doing with him. I was afraid that having notes would make the conference stilted, but I needed them to make sure I covered everything.

There's no magic formula we can share with you that will guarantee success or prevent disaster in a parent-teacher conference. But we do have some suggestions to help you get ready.

BEFORE THE CONFERENCE

Regardless of the conference's purpose—whether it's a "getting to know you" or a special meeting called to deal with a particular problem—both parent and teacher need to do some preparation before meeting face-to-face.

A mother we know tells the story of the teacher who complained that Dawn and her best friend talked all the time in class:

> "I'm at my wit's end. Do you have any ideas?" asked the teacher.
>
> "Sure," answered our friend. "I will talk to Dawn when she gets home and remind her that she ought not to be talking to her buddy in class."
>
> Then our friend played dumb and asked the teacher if he had tried separating the girls. He hadn't. Our friend said this: "I'm happy to cooperate with the teacher and take on part of the responsibility for my daughter's behavior, but really, shouldn't he have done his homework first and tried changing their seats?"

You, too, have a little homework to do before meeting with the teacher. Here are some suggestions:

Step 1. Since the conference is focused on your child, begin your preparation with her. You might want to say something like this: "I am looking forward to meeting your teacher. Mrs. Hernandez and I will be meeting on Thursday, and we'll be talking about how you're doing in school."

Step 2. Then ask your child some questions. These will tell you how she feels about school. We have always found it a good idea to get our children's permission to tell the teacher what they have told us, especially if there is a problem. If your child does not want you to share a story, *don't*. That way she knows you respect her confidence. Ask her the following:

- What are your best subjects? Why do you like these best?
- What are your worst subjects? Why don't you like these as much? Do you have trouble with these subjects?
- How do you think your teacher feels about you? What does she think about your work?
- Do you have any questions you would like me to ask your teacher?
- Is it all right if I talk with your teacher about what you've said tonight?

Step 3. If you have questions about your child's work in specific subjects or about her grades, collect some samples: homework papers, writing samples, tests, and any other things that you have questions about—and bring them with you to the conference.

Step 4. Set a realistic goal or two for yourself during the conference. In twenty or thirty minutes, you probably won't be able to discuss issues in all the curriculum areas, but you will be able to talk about one of them and maybe about homework assignments, too. A reasonable goal might be to figure out with the teacher some ways to help your child gain confidence in a particular subject and get more organized with homework assignments.

Step 5. Because you might be a little nervous during the meeting, write down some questions or facts you want to share with the teacher and determine how they relate to your goals. These are some areas you might want to cover.

- **How the teacher sees your child's work compared with expectations for the grade level:**

  How is my child doing in comparison with her classmates?

  Is she performing at, above, or below grade level in mathematics, in reading?

  Can you show me samples of her schoolwork that demonstrate this?

  What reading and math groups is she in? How did you determine this?

  Is her placement in small groups the same regardless of the subject, or is her grouping for instruction more varied?

- **The school's testing practices and policies:**

  Has my child taken any standardized tests?

  Why are these tests given, and what do they show?

  How did she do? What areas of strength and weakness were revealed?

  What can we do together to capitalize on the positive and address the negative?

- **Your child's social and emotional development as seen in school:**

  How does my child get along with her classmates?

  Does she seem eager to participate in class, or is she timid about volunteering an answer?

  Does she seem to like working in small groups?

  Is she a leader or a follower?

- **How the teacher thinks you can help your child at home:**

  Does she hand in her homework consistently? Is it done properly?

  Do you feel she needs any special help with what she is learning in school, or is homework enough?

  How can I help her?

  Does she need a tutor? If so, where might I find a good one?

- **Things you would like the teacher to know about your child**, such as her love of books about relationships, her new baby brother, her anxiety in new situations, and her ability with the violin.

DURING THE CONFERENCE

Make sure you arrive on time for the conference and leave promptly when the time is over. If you haven't finished or if there are still unresolved problems, you can make another appointment.

Right at the beginning when you and the teacher are introducing yourselves, say something that will put her at ease. Tell her that your child loves going to school—if that's true—or that the room looks cheerful and full of life or whatever is appropriate. Tell her that you have some questions and information you'd like to share with her when she's finished. If it seems appropriate or useful, tell her what your goals are.

The teacher has also prepared for the conference. Listen to her with an open mind but do interrupt if you don't understand something. You might want to tell her that you can be forgetful at times so you will be jotting down brief notes while she's talking. If she mentions areas of concern or subjects where your child needs extra help, ask her for specific suggestions about what both of you can do to help.

Then ask any of your questions that haven't been touched on. And don't miss the chance to share anything significant about your child that you feel the teacher should know. Remember to thank her for her time and interest in your child. Reiterate whatever decisions the two of you made and who will do what, and tell her that you're looking forward to working together.

AFTER THE CONFERENCE

When you get home, talk with your child about the conference in a positive way. Tell her that you liked her teacher, that the room looked great, and that you and the teacher had a good meeting. If you and the teacher formulated strategies for helping your child, tell her that you'll be working together to make sure she has a successful year in school. Let her know what some of the strategies are.

Don't gloss over any problems you discussed. Your child is probably aware of them anyway. Letting her know that you and the teacher are proud of her progress as well as concerned about her difficulties gives the message that both of you care about her and her learning.

A short thank-you note will let the teacher know you appreciate the time she gave you. It also confirms in writing your understanding of decisions made and the next steps to be taken. In the weeks that follow, look for signs that the teacher is fulfilling her part of the bargain, and make sure that you do yours. Don't hesitate to write a short note asking the teacher if she sees any improvement in your child's work. Find out if you should meet again or if you should continue what you're doing a while longer.

ONE CONFERENCE SCENARIO

To see how our advice plays out, let's look at some snippets of a real-life conference. It began painfully:

> I was devastated when I received the call from Linda's fourth-grade teacher. He was very angry and told me that Linda had been rude to him. He demanded a written apology with a promise that she wouldn't behave the same way again. I didn't know what to say; Linda had never been rude to

a teacher before. I was too shocked even to ask him any questions. I said I would speak to Linda.

An important lesson we've learned is that we don't have to react on the spot when we receive a call like the one Linda's mother did. It is okay to say to the teacher, "I need time to think about what you've said and to talk to my child. When can I get back to you?" Then we can first hear our child's side of the story and jot down our thoughts.

When my husband and I questioned Linda that night, she explained that the teacher had said something that wasn't true, and she had challenged him. He told Linda that he was the teacher, and she had no right to question him. She went on to say that the teacher was frequently rude to children who questioned him.

Clearly, this situation called for a conference immediately, given the teacher's tirade on the telephone coupled with Linda's comments to her parents. Linda's mom called the teacher and scheduled an appointment for the next morning. Her parents asked Linda if she wanted to be part of the conference, and she declined. The conference did not get off to a good start:

The next morning we went to meet with the teacher. When we got there, we told Mr. Sacco that Linda did not want to be part of the conference, and that was fine with us. He wasn't happy but agreed. Before Linda could leave, though, the teacher told her he wanted to show her that she wasn't as smart as she thought she was. He then told Linda that her score had gone down a few percentage points on a recent standardized test.

Naturally, the parents were infuriated by Mr. Sacco's comments, but they remained calm. If they had blown up, they might have felt better, and certainly their anger would have been justified. His remarks seemed to confirm Linda's version of the story, but Linda was going to be in Mr. Sacco's class for another four months, so telling him off might have made her life miserable. Instead, the parents began by clarifying what had happened to see how the teacher's description matched Linda's.

MOTHER: It would be helpful to us if you could tell us exactly what happened yesterday.

TEACHER: We're learning about explorers in social studies. When I said that Christopher Columbus discovered America, Linda shouted out, "That's not true!" She was rude, and she disputed what I said in front of the class.

FATHER: Linda questioned you and was rude to you?

TEACHER: Yes, and I don't tolerate rudeness in my class.

FATHER: I can understand your not wanting children to be rude to you.

TEACHER: I must have control in my classroom, and by questioning my authority and being rude, Linda undermined that control.

FATHER: I can see why it is important for a teacher to have control of a class and for people not to be rude.

Linda's dad used *active listening* in this conversation—something that people with good communication skills use every day. He paraphrased or repeated the problem the teacher presented; he acknowledged the teacher's strong feelings about rudeness and control of the class, and he summarized the main points. The conference continued.

MOTHER: We agree that no child should ever be rude to a teacher, and we will ask Linda to write an apology to you for her behavior.

TEACHER: I will be satisfied with that.

MOTHER: We have taught Linda to question things, however. She told us that Columbus couldn't have discovered America because there were already people living here.

TEACHER: I didn't mean it that way.

MOTHER: In fact, we believe that inquiry is an important part of education. Is there some way that you can help Linda and the other students learn the proper way to question information you present? I'm sure this would help them all. You would be doing everyone a great service.

TEACHER: I will try to teach the students a thing or two about polite questioning, but I won't accept rudeness.

Linda's parents realized that this conversation could go around in circles, and they thought it should end—but not before they said something about Mr. Sacco's inappropriate remark about Linda's standardized test scores. They played "dumb" because they believed that assertive behavior would not work with this teacher.

MOTHER: At the beginning of our conference today, you mentioned to Linda that her scores had gone down. Although this conference was called to talk about the classroom incident, do you want to talk about her test scores now, too? Or did you just bring it up to put Linda in her place?

TEACHER: That's right. I wanted to humble her a little.

MOTHER: We find that discussing a situation with Linda—its implications and consequences—is more helpful than putting her down. I'm sharing our strategy with you because it might help you in working with Linda.

FATHER: Thank you so much for your time. Linda tells us

how busy her day is, so we are grateful that you could find
time to see us. Please don't ever hesitate to call us.

Linda's parents did not compromise themselves or their
daughter in this conference. They quickly determined how
Mr. Sacco would have responded to assertiveness: He probably would have felt that he had lost control, something
that he had articulated as very important. So they swal-
lowed hard and remained calm—but got their message
across anyway. Afterward, they discussed the conference
with their daughter.

That night we talked with Linda about better ways to
question Mr. Sacco without challenging him. We explained
that her questions would be more effective if they were not
seen as impertinent. We also told her that we did not believe
in put-downs such as Mr. Sacco's comment about her test
scores. We helped Linda write her apology and enclosed it
with our own note to Mr. Sacco:

Dear Mr. Sacco,

We would like to thank you again for meeting with us so
quickly after we called to schedule an appointment.

We were glad to have the opportunity to talk about the
incident in the classroom. We've talked with Linda a little
about more appropriate ways to ask questions and have
told her that you will be giving all the students more advice
about this soon.

Thank you.

A SECOND CONFERENCE SCENARIO

Not every conference is as difficult as that one. Let's look at another scenario. This one also began with some anxiety for the parent; conferences usually do.

MOTHER: I was excited and a little bit nervous about meeting Chrissy's teacher. My daughter had been an *A* student before we moved to this community because of my job, and now Chrissy was doing *B* work. I felt awful that her marks had gone down and requested the conference. I was worried that the move had affected her grades, but I really didn't know.

In this case, however, the teacher was much more sensitive to the parent's feelings and was able to get the conference off to a good start.

TEACHER: I could tell that Chrissy's mom was anxious about our appointment the minute she introduced herself to me. I considered myself lucky to have her daughter in my class and told her so right away. It seemed to put her at ease.

Then I asked Mrs. Weaver to tell me in some detail why she was worried about Chrissy. Because I feel it's very important for a teacher to know as much as he can about the students in his class, I also asked a lot of questions about her reading habits, friendships, relationships with her siblings, and her perception of her new school and class.

Her mother reported that Chrissy, like the other fourth graders, was devouring Nancy Drew books, had typical love/hate relationships with her younger brothers, and seemed to have adjusted to the move quite well. She didn't have as many friends yet as she did at her old school, but then again, they had been in town only about four weeks.

After eliciting information from her mother, Mr. Brown shared his own perceptions. Because he had spent time observing Chrissy and thinking about her adjustment, he had some specific ideas to offer.

MOTHER: It felt good to talk to Mr. Brown about Chrissy. I was delighted and impressed that he was so interested. No other teacher had ever asked as many questions about my children as he did. I wasn't able to tell him much about Chrissy's perceptions of her new school or of her place in his class. She shrugged off every one of my questions about school with a simple "Everything's fine."
TEACHER: I told Mrs. Weaver that Chrissy was doing well in my class, which contained more than its share of very bright students. She was a little timid about answering questions and didn't seem to like to read out loud. From what I had observed, she was as bright as her peers but was a little nervous about taking risks in her new environment. The nervousness caused her to withdraw and not volunteer her opinion. I told Mrs. Weaver that I thought once Chrissy became more comfortable with her peers, she would open up and participate more in class. Once I saw more class participation and more effort on Chrissy's part, I would raise her marks to A.

The conference closed with parent and teacher trading ideas about how to help Chrissy and agreeing to check with each other again soon. The mother who began this meeting feeling anxious left feeling completely reassured after this nearly ideal parent-teacher conference.

MOTHER: I asked Mr. Brown what I could do to help Chrissy feel more comfortable in class. He gave me the names of children she was friendly with and suggested I encourage Chrissy to make play dates with them. He also suggested that I press her to talk about the class and her classwork. In fact, he gave me some ideas about what to say to Chrissy to get her to open up. And then he asked me what I thought! I asked him if he could put Chrissy together with a few kids to do a cooperative project. That might help break the ice, I thought. He said he thought it was a great idea and promised to begin the next day.

TEACHER: I assured Mrs. Weaver that I was not worried about Chrissy. I thought she was just having a typical reaction to the move, and I was sure she would be okay soon. We promised to be in touch with each other in a month to assess the situation. I thanked Mrs. Weaver for making the appointment to speak with me.

MOTHER: I was so relieved after meeting with Mr. Brown. The next time I speak to him I won't be so nervous. He didn't make me feel stupid; he took my concerns seriously, and he didn't treat me like a pushy parent. Best of all, he obviously cared about Chrissy and had spent time thinking about her. We're going to have a great year!

IF YOU'RE NOT SATISFIED

As you might have suspected, Linda's parents in our first scenario were not completely satisfied after meeting with Mr. Sacco. While the immediate problem was more or less resolved by the conference, the larger issue of Mr. Sacco's inability to deal with children questioning him was not. Further, although Linda did apologize, her parents feared that Mr. Sacco might continue to treat her and other students badly.

The next logical step was to meet with the principal. They were worried, however, that this might result in even worse treatment for Linda. Many parents experience this dilemma: They know that if they don't go to the principal, she won't know about the problem. But if they do, the teacher might be offended and take it out on their child. Unfortunately, teachers have been known to do just that.

A third alternative is to go to the principal "anonymously," on the condition that she doesn't tell the teacher who complained. This is what Linda's parents decided to do. They met with the principal and told her their story. The principal followed up with Mr. Sacco by dropping in on the classroom several times to keep an eye on what was happening there.

Sometimes, unfortunately, even the principal won't be able to effect a change in a teacher's behavior. If the situation is very bad, you might consider asking for your child to be transferred to another class. Before you take this step, however, find out your child's feelings about leaving her friends, and weigh those feelings very carefully. Both of us have considered this alternative but have been reluctant to take it—in large part because of our children's unwillingness to leave their classmates. If you decide to proceed, remember that this might not be easy. If there are problems with the teacher, many other parents might be requesting transfers, too. Obviously, the principal will find it impossible to grant everyone's request.

Each of our children has been in the class of a not-so-good teacher at some point. When this happens, we take all the steps we can think of to safeguard our child's self-esteem and to ensure that academic learning takes place. We meet with the teacher often, follow up on the meetings, volunteer to help in the classroom or on trips as many times as we can, alert other schoolpeople whom we trust that there's a problem, and try to stay on top of what's happening from week to week.

And we do something else that's very important: We use these opportunities to help our children learn to deal with difficult people. We reassure them that they are valuable and competent even if the teacher doesn't see it, and we talk about how we have learned to work with difficult people on our jobs or in other parts of our lives. As a result, we have both seen our children grow in self-confidence and in the ability to adapt to unpleasant circumstances—skills that will stand them in good stead as adults.

4

THE THREE Rs AT HOME AND AT SCHOOL

Ask us when the next PTA meeting is or whether our children do their homework or when the weekly social studies quiz is given, and we can tell you in a flash. But ask us what fifth graders study in science or when long division is introduced, and we don't have a clue. That's okay. It's not our job to know the details of the curriculum; it's the teacher's. To be effective in our roles as supporters and teachers of our children, we need to understand the basic concepts, skills, and approaches of each curriculum area. In this chapter, we provide a taste of these, followed by suggestions for at-home activities.

You might be confused about the distinction between *curriculum* and *instruction*. We often have been. When we use the term *curriculum* here, we mean the content of our children's studies; *instruction* is the way the teacher helps them learn.

Most parents are not in a position to evaluate curriculum, but we can raise important questions based on observations of our children and discussions with other parents. When we see something we don't like or understand, then we can ask questions such as these:

• Does the curriculum seem to rely on memorization of facts and figures to the exclusion of critical thinking or problem-solving skills? Do children have opportunities to approach the subject matter creatively?
• Does any one subject seem to be getting short shrift?
• Are certain topics, such as AIDS or child abuse, being handled in a way we consider appropriate?
• Are language and communication skills developed in all curriculum areas, or are they confined to the language arts period?

The importance of raising questions can be seen in the story of John Mendez, the parent of a fourth grader:

John made a habit of reviewing his daughter's homework every night when he got home from work. One November he realized that he had seen no homework in science and asked Jennifer about this. "We hardly ever do any science," Jennifer said.

This worried John, who began his research by calling the superintendent's office and inquiring about a curriculum outline (or syllabus, as it's often called) of fourth-grade science. The superintendent's secretary directed him to the district science coordinator, who asked him why he wanted a copy. Not wanting to cause trouble prematurely, John said that he had a child in fourth grade and was interested in what she would be learning in science. The coordinator mailed him a copy.

John reviewed it carefully and asked Jennifer some pointed questions about areas the outline indicated should have been covered. "Dad, we don't spend as much time on

science as we did last year. And we didn't learn that stuff!"
Jennifer insisted.

John then faced the dilemma of questioning school authority. Neither a teacher nor a scientist, he could still see
that Jennifer and her classmates were being shortchanged.
They weren't getting what the district's own curriculum
outline said they should be getting.

"I knew I had to do something," John told us, "so I called
the school and made an appointment with the teacher."
His meeting with her was friendly. She readily admitted
she wasn't doing much science. "I have so much to cover
in class that is more important," she told John. "And I
don't really like science that much. But I promise I'll try
to catch up."

John waited two weeks, observed the homework, and
talked to Jennifer. He didn't see any change, so he made
an appointment with the principal. John was afraid that
this was going to be a difficult meeting. The principal should
have been aware that the teacher wasn't following the syllabus; one reason for having a curriculum outline is to give
principals a tool for assessing whether the teacher is covering the subject matter sufficiently. Sometimes there are
good reasons for not keeping up with the outline—if the
students aren't ready for the material or if they have needs
in another area that must take precedence. Neither was the
case here, however. John was anxious going into the meeting, knowing that he wasn't an expert and might encounter
some defensiveness.

John simply told the principal his story, from initial observations of Jennifer's homework through meeting with the

teacher and afterward. "It's good that you brought this to my attention," said the principal. "I spoke to Jennifer's teacher yesterday after you called to make the appointment. She confirms your perception that they're not doing enough science. We worked out a schedule of class visits by the district science coordinator, who will team teach with her to help the class catch up and make a plan for the rest of the year."

This ending to John's story was the best possible scenario. We've heard about similar stories where principals and teachers were very defensive. If that happens to you, you should probably go to the next highest level, to an assistant superintendent of curriculum and instruction or to the superintendent.

Sometimes situations like these end badly because the parent is not as sensitive or as thorough as John was. Our advice is to stay calm and take one step at a time. Don't rush to the principal before talking with the teacher, and try to see the problem from the schoolpeople's perspective.

In this case, despite the "happy" ending, John remained diligent, reviewing Jennifer's homework and checking to see what she did in class. He also supplemented the school-work with at-home activities such as the ones we suggest in the following pages.

READING AND LANGUAGE ARTS

Do you remember when children were taught reading, writing, and spelling as separate and distinct subjects? We're sorry to say that's still taking place in thousands of schools all over the country.

In these schools, the teacher asks the children to take

out their spelling books. She identifies ten words and asks students to look them up in a dictionary, write their definitions, and use the words in sentences. The children spend some time on geography next, and maybe an hour later they are asked to open their readers. They take turns reading aloud one of the stories in the book, perhaps in small groups.

In contrast, teachers in an increasing number of schools understand that everything kids learn in school requires a combination of reading, writing, speaking, and listening skills, and they work to develop these skills throughout the school day. Reading, spelling, and vocabulary are not taught as separate entities but are integrated in all the subject areas to help students increase all their language skills. This is sometimes called the *whole language* approach.

A typical day in a school with such an integrated language arts program might be like this:

The morning begins with a social studies lesson on the westward expansion. Rather than read from the history textbook, the teacher asks students to read a chapter or two in *Little House on the Prairie*, a story set in those times. He then divides the class into groups and assigns each group the responsibility of working together to answer one of five questions based on what they read. Each group is directed to write their responses to his questions in whole sentences and to keep a separate list of unfamiliar vocabulary words. He then asks one of the children in each group to report to the class on the group's work. After this, he takes out a map of America and asks the children to show him the location of the story.

A great deal of good instruction is going on in this teacher's class. The most important is that reading is integrated;

it's not separate from everything else. The teacher weaves reading into social studies, geography and map skills, oral communication, and writing. When different subject areas (disciplines) are combined like this, it's called *interdisciplinary*. This teacher also uses different kinds of groupings to accomplish some of his lesson goals for the morning. (See Chapter 6 where we discuss these.)

WHAT YOU CAN DO

Supporting your child's language development is probably one of the most important things you'll do as a parent. In a nutshell, all the expert advice comes down to this: *Talk, talk, talk. Read, read, read. Listen, listen, listen.* When language is a rich part of your everyday lives, your child won't have any difficulty learning to read. Here are some specific ideas:

• Discuss things—anything!—with your child: the lengthening days, the sounds of the cicadas, the colors of cars going by.
• Read everything together: street signs, cereal boxes, movie titles.
• Continue reading books together aloud even when your child can read by himself.
• If you're reading a book with many chapters over several days, read one chapter a night. Before going on to the next one, ask your child to recount what you read the night before.
• When she's very young, read your child a story and ask her to retell it to you in her own words. Or in the middle of a story, ask her to predict what will happen next.
• Go to the library regularly and encourage your son to choose his own books.

• Watch television together and talk about what you've seen.

• Look for simple recipes and plan a special meal with your child. If he can, let him write the shopping list. If he's not writing yet, have him draw pictures of what you need for the meal. And when you're at the supermarket, read the labels on the cans, bottles, and boxes to him. Finally, cook the meal together and enjoy!

• Take out a subscription to a children's magazine for your child. (Some good ones are *Ranger Rick, Highlights for Children*, and *National Geographic World*.) It will be fun for her to get mail every few weeks.

• Surprise your child with a short note in his lunch box or next to his breakfast cereal bowl.

• Let your child help you plan your vacation. Look at maps together and talk about what you need to bring on the trip. A scrapbook or a journal of the trip would be a great activity to do together when it's over.

• Encourage your child to write letters to grandparents or friends who don't live nearby. Give him a bunch of magic markers to decorate the letter. The recipients will surely express their gratitude, your child's self-esteem will be boosted, and this will encourage him to write more.

MATHEMATICS

Math gives us tools for organizing and quantifying things in the world around us. Arithmetic, as we used to call it, is the most elementary branch of mathematics: computation. In the early years, from kindergarten through sixth grade, most youngsters learn the basic mathematical tools. First, they learn to count. They begin to learn the language of math, including terms such as *greater than* and *equal to*.

They sort and classify using concrete objects such as rods, coins, or toys—creating sets by size or color or some other characteristic. Once they have mastered these skills, they learn to add, subtract, multiply, and divide, at first only with whole numbers. Gradually they extend the four operations to fractions, decimals, and percentages. They also work with money, time, weight, and three-dimensional space (size and shape). Through all of these experiences the emphasis is on manipulating concrete objects. For elementary school youngsters, math involves the real world. They are learning to solve problems by interpreting information and then using the appropriate mathematical notations and operations. Some teachers now post the multiplication tables on the board or pass out calculators —something you would never have seen when we were in school. Their intent is to deemphasize rote memorization and focus attention on the process instead. Not only in math but in other subjects, too, the process of what the children are doing—how it works and why—is now considered most significant.

In the secondary grades (seven to twelve), mathematical operations are more sophisticated and abstract. Sometimes it's hard to see any connection to the real world at all in some of the advanced courses, such as trigonometry and calculus. But the four basic operations and the same problem-solving skills are still part of what students do.

Many students develop math anxiety: They are afraid of it and are convinced that they can't do it. Studies have shown that math anxiety is especially prevalent among girls and minorities, who tend to be underrepresented in advanced math courses. Organizations such as Educational Equity Concepts, Inc., and the Women's Educational Equity Act Publishing Center are working hard to abolish math anxiety.

WHAT YOU CAN DO

We parents can help prevent our children from "catching" math anxiety. If we suffered from it ourselves, we need to be especially on guard not to pass it on. Here are some very simple things you can do:

• Play number games with your child. Most of us are aware of how important it is for us to read to our children from an early age. It's just as important for us to start early with numbers. Count the fire hydrants you pass, add up pennies spread out on the table, or play games like "This Little Piggie . . ." These simple activities can help show our children that math is fun and that it makes sense.

• Play board games such as Sorry and Monopoly. These require math skills and can be a great way to have fun with your child.

• Play the "paper clip counting game" with your child. It's easy: Place twelve paper clips on the table and ask her to separate them into two (or three or four) equal piles. Encourage her to talk about her reasons for dividing the clips into the piles she did. Then make it more complicated; take one clip away and ask her to divide the clips into two unequal piles, one with one more clip than the other. Vary the game.

• Give your child a yardstick and ask him to measure five items around the house. Ask him to write down the measurements and put the items in order from the smallest to the largest.

• Cook with your child. This is always a good way to combine fun and learning. Have your son help you make a batch of fudge. He can see the relationship between one-half and one-quarter cup when he helps you measure the cocoa and the confectioner's sugar. He'll learn the concepts of *less than* and *equal to*, and he'll see practical applications of the fractions he's learned in school.

• Ask your daughter to count to one hundred by twos, then by fives and by tens.

SOCIAL STUDIES

It's no accident that the current social studies curriculum reflects what education's founders had in mind when they started the first public schools. The concept of *citizenship*, introduced as early as kindergarten, is at the core of everything our children study in this discipline during their thirteen years in school.

Other concepts introduced in the early elementary grades become broader as our children get older and incorporate more and more experiences into their world. Personal identity, interdependence, the environment, government, culture, technology, and diversity are all integrated into a well-rounded social studies curriculum.

Skills such as problem solving, analysis, and decision making—frequently referred to as *critical thinking skills*—and research, information gathering, and the interpersonal skills of respect and responsibility have replaced the more traditional emphasis on memorizing dates and events.

Let's follow the concept of citizenship and see how it develops. We start with an example of its introduction in kindergarten, then use a sixth grader's experience to describe it halfway through his schooling. We end with a description of a high school social studies elective.

Two children are building with blocks in the corner of a kindergarten classroom. One child is building a ranch-style home similar to the one he lives in while another child is working on a five-story apartment house not unlike her home. Along comes a third child who kicks down both buildings. The builders are understandably upset.

The teacher uses this experience to engage these children and the rest of the class in a discussion about the rights of the individual and societal expectations. Together they develop some fundamental rules of the classroom, such as, "We look but we don't touch." It's the beginning of citizenship instruction.

Johnny's sixth-grade social studies and language arts teachers tried an interdisciplinary or integrated approach to teach the relationships between our government's past history, our present form of government, and our responsibility as citizens.

Selected readings from autobiographies of some early leaders began the investigation of history. The readings provoked a conversation about the frustrations involved in establishing a government. Soon the teachers moved the conversation to a discussion about how the school was governed. The students then began a lengthy project that resulted in the formation of their own student organization.

Students in some high schools serve as judge and jury, deciding the fate of their peers who break school rules. Training is provided to the students in social studies classes before they earn the right to participate in this mock court. Faculty in schools that have student-run court systems find the students are much harder on their peers than the administrators who typically dispense punishments.

WHAT YOU CAN DO

There are many ways to enrich your child's understanding of social studies concepts at home.

• Read the newspaper or watch television news together and discuss current events. Your knowledge and opinions about what's going on in the world add an important dimension to your child's developing values.

• Talk about upcoming elections—who is running, what the issues are, whom you're voting for and why. If your child is young, take her with you to vote. We found that our children, when very young, loved to pull the lever once we had made our choices in the voting booth. The only difficulty was keeping them from trying to peek behind other people's curtains.

• When it's close to a national holiday, such as Martin Luther King, Jr.'s birthday, engage your child in a conversation about the significance of the person being honored. Go to the library with your child and find out some interesting facts about the person that are not generally known.

SCIENCE

According to the dictionary, science is "systematic knowledge of the physical or material world." In school it also involves thinking strategies, problem solving, and ways of gathering and interpreting knowledge. In today's world, living responsibly on our planet and with one another involves making many decisions about matters related to science.

Often, in the elementary grades, not enough time is devoted to science. This is too bad because science is perfectly matched with young children's developmental interests and needs. It's almost entirely based on "hands-on" activities, enabling kids to learn by discovery. The activities are usually very concrete as well. Children use a magnet with various objects to discover what happens, for example, and then make their own generalizations about what they observe. The key concept is *interaction*: What happens when I do this or when I put this with that? Elementary school science activities use objects and experiences in the child's immediate world; they are geared to observing, exploring, asking questions, and discovering answers, rather than reading textbooks or listening to lectures.

In the secondary grades, science is usually broken down into different subjects: biology, chemistry, physics, earth science. Concepts become more abstract, and activities include reading, experimentation, discussion, and application—the more formal kinds of discovery and reasoning that form the basis of the scientific method.

WHAT YOU CAN DO

You're probably thinking that you aren't equipped to help your child with science. But you are. The key is letting your child experiment and observe the results.

Here are a few examples of what you can do:

- Fill a measuring cup with snow and then leave it on the counter to melt. Note the amount of water compared with the amount of snow. Help your child figure out the reason for the discrepancy. (The cup is half-full with water because the air trapped in the snow is released when it melts.)
- Make some steam together. Put water in a pan on the stove and wait for it to boil. Then point out the steam—now a gas—that escapes into the air.
- Experiment by filling a bowl with tap water and sprinkling pepper on the surface. Touch the water with the tip of a bar of soap and watch what happens.

- Watch a National Geographic special or another nature program on television and discuss it together.
- Family visits to the zoo, explorations in the backyard, cooking and baking with your child, and even playing in the bathtub can be turned into science activities. Remember that whenever you explore, observe, and experiment with physical objects, that's science!

FOREIGN LANGUAGES

Our children are beginning to learn other languages earlier than ever before. In fact, the study of a foreign language is no longer reserved for high school and college. As our country becomes increasingly multicultural, the need for our children to learn other languages is obvious. While some students are learning Spanish, French, or Latin as early as the first grade, most school districts start foreign language instruction in Spanish, Italian, and French in the middle or junior high schools. German, Russian, Japanese, and Chinese are offered in some schools but usually only in larger school districts.

If you and other parents believe that foreign language instruction should begin in the fourth grade and your school district doesn't offer it, you can try to persuade your principal to make it part of the curriculum. Because of the budget constraints that schools always face, it won't be easy, but you might be able to find a compromise.

One group of parents we read about approached their children's principal with this very idea. They asked him to consider offering Spanish to their children, stating, "Our school is fifty percent Latino, and we English-speaking parents feel it is very important that our children learn the language of their classmates." The principal concurred and submitted a proposal to the district superintendent. Although funding was not available for a full-time teacher, there was enough to support a teacher for a few hours a week in an after-school program. It wasn't exactly what the parents wanted, but it was a start.

WHAT YOU CAN DO

You are probably wondering how you can help your child at home when the last time you uttered a word in Spanish or French was in your junior year of high school or as a freshman in college. Don't worry! Like foreign language instruction, our suggested activities are intended to broaden our children's awareness of the peoples and cultures of the world around them.

• Give your child a few magazines, a pair of scissors, and some glue and paper. Ask him to cut out pictures of countries in which English is not the dominant language. Tell him to look for the country in the dictionary if he's not sure what language is spoken there. He can write that down next to the picture.
• Encourage your children to try the foods of other countries. While doing so, talk with them about the culture and the people of the country.
• Check your local children's bookstore or library for language-learning tapes and books in other languages written for children. A tape of familiar songs in Spanish, for example, teaches the language in an easy and fun way. You can learn (or refresh your memory) right alongside your child.

PHYSICAL EDUCATION AND HEALTH EDUCATION

Gym is always a favorite subject, especially in the elementary school years when children need to run around and let off steam. It's also mandatory in most states.

Physical education usually begins with simple games and, like academic subjects, gets more complex as children grow. Rules get more complicated, the motor skills more demanding, and the emphasis on teamwork more pronounced. A good physical education program enhances social as well as physical development as youngsters learn to be part of a team and experience both winning and losing.

In addition, many different health education programs are now included under the physical education umbrella. Curricula designed to teach children how to avoid drug and alcohol abuse, AIDS, and child abuse and to help them develop healthy and informed attitudes about sex and family life are all apt to be found here. These vary across districts and especially across states, so check to see which are offered by your child's school.

WHAT YOU CAN DO

There are many ways to enhance your child's physical development as well as her attitudes toward her own health. Chances are that you're already doing this, but just in case you need a few more ideas, here are some:

• Encourage your child to join a sports team. Many towns have recreation departments that sponsor a wide range of children's sports—from soccer to basketball to ice skating.

At little or no cost, your child can have the fun of learning a sport and competing on a team, and you'll get to know other parents at the games. Some of our closest friendships began on the sidelines of Sunday afternoon soccer matches. And our kids developed a lifelong (we hope!) love of physical activity.

• Play catch in the backyard, shoot baskets against the garage, or pitch a few balls to your fledgling ball player. When our children were very young, we found that playing sports with them was fun, and it encouraged their participation.

• Take regular walks together. Research suggests that a brisk walk several times a week pays off in tremendous dividends to your health. After dinner or early in the morning—whichever time is best for your family—walk the dog, walk to the park, or just walk around the neighborhood. You may find that this time together becomes more and more precious as your child gets older. And it's good for you!

• Involve your child in planning meals. Reading recipes and labels not only improves reading skills, it also increases awareness of what we eat and what's good for us. In busy lives, moreover, it's always nice to have an extra pair of hands in the kitchen.

• Watch television specials about health issues and talk about them afterward. There are some good, informative programs these days about everything from teen pregnancy to drug abuse that we can watch with our children. Sometimes a TV program makes it easier to start talking about a difficult subject.

THE ARTS

Learning to sing, to play an instrument, and to create visual statements are important skills. In all of the arts, children are encouraged to express their own ideas rather than to give back "right" answers. Sometimes this is a place for children who aren't successful in other areas to shine. But the arts require discipline, too; the violin sings only after long hours of practice.

The arts also provide a perfect opportunity to make English literature, language, or social studies come alive. Remember when you studied the Civil War? You probably learned about it from a textbook. When music and art are integrated in the curriculum, the war might come alive through listening to Negro spirituals or by viewing and discussing a broad spectrum of the paintings or photographs of the time.

We wish every child had these opportunities; due to the always limited budgets of schools, however, that just isn't the case. Sometimes the PTA can fund after-school or lunchtime arts classes or sponsor artist-in-residence programs to make the arts a bigger presence in the school.

WHAT YOU CAN DO

There are so many things that we as parents can do to foster and encourage our children's interest in the arts. The activities we suggest are not limited to families who live in or near big cities; they are possible for families in small and large towns throughout the country.

• Ask your children if they would like to take art or music lessons. Look in the Yellow Pages or talk to friends and schoolpeople to find out where lessons are being offered. Before signing them up, however, make sure you explain to them what kind of commitment they will have to make. All of our children have had music lessons. Laurette's son stopped because the commitment interfered with his soccer time, and her daughter stopped because the teacher had placed unreasonable demands on her. She was in fourth grade, and the teacher wanted her to practice for one and a half hours a night! She wasn't a budding virtuoso, and that was too much. As we've said elsewhere, balance is important. Diane's daughter still loves her violin lessons and is willing to commit the extra time.

• Visiting an art museum can be an enjoyable way to spend a Saturday or Sunday with your child. We've learned three lessons about taking our children to museums: Make the visit short, visit only one section of the museum on each trip, and do a little homework beforehand. Believe us, it will make the visit more enjoyable and worthwhile.

For example, get a children's library book on a particular artist, and make it your reading material the week before your visit. Look at pictures of the artist's work and discuss them. It pays off! Laurette's son once loudly exclaimed in the quiet museum, "Wow, I didn't realize from the book we read that Jackson Pollock's paintings were so gigantic!"

• Attend performances of mimes, dancers, story tellers, and theater groups geared to young children. While some of these might be costly, others run by nonprofit groups and high school and college performing arts clubs are not so dear. Prepare your child for the performance and talk about it later over a dish of frozen yogurt.

• Introduce your child to music through records, tapes, and CDs borrowed from the library. When he's old enough, encourage your son to start his own music library and teach him how to take care of it. Include a wide range of selections from classical music—Tchaikovsky's *Peter and the Wolf* is a great beginning—to folk music (local as well as international) to children's music.

- Put together an art box for your child, perhaps in a large cardboard box that she decorates. Include all sorts of goodies: magic markers, colored pencils, construction and tissue paper, a ream of cheap duplicating paper, a box of water paints, glue, glitter, string, yarn, pencils, scissors, cotton balls, paint brushes, rubber stamps and colored stamp pads, and last but not least, a giant box of crayons. You can start this box with just a few items when your children are very young and add more sophisticated items as they get older. Remember to establish some rules about where the items can be used. If you have no room in the kitchen and have to use the dining room or bedroom, you might want to include a plastic tablecloth or shower curtain to protect your furniture and floors.

THE EXTRAS

Computers, field trips, assembly programs, and extracurricular activities provide opportunities for teachers to reinforce and extend the basics. Unfortunately, in some school districts, when the school board is looking for places to pare the budget, they start with these. Thus, while almost every district has some of these "extras," the specifics can vary a great deal. You'll want to learn which opportunities are available in your child's school.

COMPUTERS

In some districts, computers are a way of life for students from kindergarten through high school. Our children use them as comfortably as we used pens and pencils during our school days.

"User friendly" computers and software do more than prepare kids for a computer-literate world, although that's an important benefit. They also promote critical thinking skills, such as problem solving and decision making; provide drill and practice of the concepts learned in other subjects, such as math; allow students access to databases outside the school; and enable them to network with students in other grades, schools, and even countries. In addition, their word processing capability is a boon for students for whom writing is difficult. "My child disliked writing because he hated to print or write cursive, but he loved to tell stories," one mother told us. "The computer saved his life. He could quickly spin tales on the keyboard and then go back and make corrections easily."

Sooner or later the topic of buying a computer will come up in your family. Don't rush into this, especially if it would be a financial strain. At least until middle school, our children didn't really need a computer at home. Even then, it wasn't absolutely necessary. If you do want to buy one, check into what the school is using and try to get one that's compatible. To help your child learn word processing, look into programs designed to teach keyboarding. Most school systems don't teach this until the sixth or seventh grade.

FIELD TRIPS

In many school districts, children go on several field trips every year, starting in kindergarten. These are usually designed to supplement what they're learning in school. Thus, classroom study of endangered species might culminate in a trip to the zoo or a natural history museum, or learning songs in music class might lead to a concert by the local orchestra in a concert hall. The idea is to take learning out of the classroom and into the world. Well-planned, well-handled field trips can add immeasurably to your child's education.

But notice we said "well-planned" and "well-handled" trips. There's nothing worse than a trip for which children are not prepared. A trip to the planetarium can be a disaster, for example, if the children don't know anything about the stars or how a planetarium works. It's dark in there, which is a perfect opportunity for all sorts of misbehavior by unprepared and bored youngsters. Children who know what to expect and who understand what the show is all about will enjoy this trip so much more, and so will the adults escorting them! If you have expertise in this area and you discover nothing has been done, volunteer to help.

One mother tells this story:

> On the trip to the Museum of Natural History, ours was the only class that didn't lose any children! Of course, the others were all found eventually, after much anxiety and running around. What was so wonderful about our class was that the children understood how important it was to stay with their parent leaders, and they watched out for one another. And that's because the teacher had spent time before the trip preparing them for it—not just for what they would see and do but also for how they should behave. So they behaved well. It was that simple.

If your child is going on a field trip, you will be asked to sign a permission slip allowing her to travel by bus or train or even to walk somewhere off the school grounds. Before you sign it, you might want to make sure that the permission slip or accompanying letter explains the destination of the trip, its purpose, how students will get there, the duration of the trip, and what alternative care arrangements will be made for children who do not go on the trip. Offer to accompany your child's class on a trip if you can. This would be an excellent use of your time. In addition to having fun with your child and her friends, going on an outing with the class gives you an opportunity to observe firsthand how your child relates to her peers, how the teacher talks to students, how students relate to one another, and how the class functions as a unit outside the classroom. All this reveals a lot about what goes on inside the classroom and will also help you appreciate the challenges your child's teacher faces every day.

ASSEMBLY PROGRAMS

Often sponsored by the parent-teacher association, school assembly programs also aim to enhance the curriculum. A child studying the four basic food groups in health education, for example, is more likely to remember the lesson if he attends an assembly where giant fruits and vegetables dance across the stage. And a drug education lesson will have more impact if the local police department presents a "show and tell" program for impressionable youngsters.

EXTRACURRICULAR ACTIVITIES

Held after school or during lunch, extracurricular activities offer students opportunities to explore talents and interests beyond the basics. While they're sometimes funded by the district, more frequently it is the PTA, the local Y, or the Recreation Department that supports them. In elementary and middle schools, some activities might include a chess club, a computer graphics class, a great books group, or open sports activities.

FURTHER READING

Daniel Coleman, Paul Kaufman, and Michael Ray. *The Creative Spirit*. New York: Dutton, 1992.

Elizabeth Crary. *Kids Can Cooperate: A Practical Guide to Teaching Problem Solving*. Seattle: Parenting Press, 1984.

Susan K. Perry. *Playing Smart: A Parent's Guide to Enriching, Offbeat Learning Activities for Ages 4–14*. Minneapolis: Free Spirit Publishing, 1990.

Tom and Harriet Sobol. *Your Child in School: Kindergarten Through Second Grade*. New York: Morrow, 1988.

———. *The Intermediate Years: Grades Three Through Five*. New York: Arbor House, 1987.

LANGUAGE AND READING

Peggy Kaye. *Games for Reading*. New York: Pantheon Books, 1984.

Jim Trelease. *The New Read-Aloud Handbook*. New York: Penguin Books, 1989.

Roger Young. *Learning to Read in the '90s: An Interactive Playbook*. Berkeley, CA: Celestial Arts, 1992.

MATHEMATICS

Marilyn Burns. *The I Hate Mathematics! Book*. Boston: Little, Brown, 1975.

———. *Math for Smarty Pants*. Boston: Little, Brown, 1982.

Peggy Kaye. *Games for Math*. New York: Pantheon Books, 1987.

Jean Kerr Stenmark, Virginia Thompson, and Ruth Cossey. *Family Math*. Berkeley, CA: Lawrence Hall of Science, 1986.

SCIENCE

Joseph Cornell. *Sharing Nature with Children*. Nevada City, CA: Dawn Publications, 1979.

John Elkington, Julia Hailes, Douglas Hill, and Joel Makower. *Going Green: A Kid's Handbook for Saving the Planet*. New York: Puffin Books, 1990.

Don Herbert. *Mr. Wizard's Supermarket Science*. New York: Random House, 1980.

Sara Stein. *The Science Book*. New York: Workman Publishing, 1979.

5

SURVIVING HOMEWORK

Homework is often the cause of conflicts between parents and children. We also find it to be the focus of the most questions at open school night every year. And it probably provokes more anxiety than any other school issue. Why? The number-one reason, we think, is that homework is misunderstood by teachers, parents, and children alike. Since homework is here to stay, we think it makes sense to sort out its purposes and to spell out appropriate roles for us to play as parents.

You are both supporter and at-home teacher when you help your children with their homework. Finding the right balance between just enough and not too much of both these roles is tricky. You don't want to take over the teacher's rightful job, yet you don't want to step so far into the background that you don't know what's going on with your child's schoolwork.

When we talk about homework, we don't just mean the nightly assignments to solve a series of math problems, complete a worksheet, and read a chapter. We also include long-term assignments such as book reports, research papers, art projects, dioramas, and the like. The amount and frequency of nightly as well as long-term homework will vary from teacher to teacher, sometimes by quite a bit.

How long should homework take? That's a question only your child's teacher can answer. Ask at open school night in the fall, write a note to the teacher, or read the letters she sends home; these might give you a rough idea of her expectations. There are some fairly consistent rules of thumb, however. Some people think ten minutes multiplied by the grade level is appropriate; therefore, expect roughly ten minutes of homework in grade one and fifty minutes in grade five. Others round this off to say that for grades one to three, twenty to thirty minutes makes sense; for grades four to six, thirty to sixty minutes.

In the families we know, it's safe to say that most kids hate homework, and most parents do, too. For the kids, the prime reason is that homework cuts into their leisure time. In addition, as the load gets heavier in middle school and high school, homework can actually cause academic burnout. Sometimes it fosters cheating, as young people feel more and more pressure to do well. And it can increase the disparity between high-achieving students, whose parents are usually available to help them, and low-achieving students, who might not have that kind of support at home.

We parents hate homework because it causes conflict and creates negative attitudes about school. Even worse, it confuses us about our own role as well as that of the teacher. We're never quite sure how carefully to check the homework or whether to force our children to correct it. (These, too, are questions to ask the teacher.) The following conversation, or one like it, may become familiar to you (if it has not already!).

MOTHER: Tommy, I cannot check your homework. I can't read it because your handwriting is so sloppy. Please take out a clean piece of paper and rewrite these sentences neatly.

CHILD: Mom, I don't want to do the sentences over. I think they're neat enough. Besides, Mr. Salvaggio doesn't care if our work is sloppy as long as he can read it.

MOTHER: It is important to me that you submit work to your teacher that is neat and legible. Please do your work again.

We think Tommy's mom did the right thing here by demanding that he meet a certain standard. Some parents might disagree, believing that Tommy will learn better if he has to face the consequences of his own choices. We don't disagree with that argument in theory; it's just that both of us have found teachers' standards to vary so much that we prefer to set our own.

Unfortunately, there are no simple answers to homework dilemmas like this one. Your child's needs and your time constraints are unique, so choose those of our suggestions that suit you.

WHY HOMEWORK?

If its purpose is not to drive us crazy, drive a wedge between us and our children, or make them feel negative about school, what are the reasons for homework? After researching this question, we've gained a new respect for the value of thoughtfully assigned homework. Its possibilities for enriching your child's education are surprisingly far-reaching.

SOME REASONS FOR HOMEWORK

All too often, homework is assigned simply because it's
expected by students, parents, and teachers. That's not a
good enough reason for us. Nor do we think that homework
can ever substitute for good teaching, but it can and should
give children an opportunity to practice what they've
learned in school and to reinforce both new and old skills.
Drill and practice assignments—doing fifteen similar math
problems, for example—are especially good at this.

Creative homework assignments can expand and enrich
the curriculum. Writing a paragraph about how it might
have felt to live in New York City during the Revolutionary
War, for example, can help to bring the "dry" facts of
history alive.

Homework can also help children become better readers
since virtually every assignment involves some reading. You
can reinforce this skill by making sure your child reads the
directions carefully, and you might want to follow the advice
one of us was given when our child was in second grade:
On evenings without homework, encourage your child to
read for at least fifteen minutes.

In addition, homework can be an application of what
students have learned in school. For spelling homework,
students can be asked to write sentences or a paragraph
showing the words' meanings. This kind of homework is a
way for teachers to evaluate what has been learned in school
and to identify what needs further attention. One teacher
told us,

I've been teaching for twenty years. Every year at open
house, I ask parents not to correct their children's work.
I want to see the mistakes in order to know where they need

further help. And every year I continue to get homework that smacks of too much parent involvement.

In the best of all worlds, homework complements the work done in school. It can also show children real connections between classroom learning and the world outside. When the class is learning to make bar graphs, for example, a useful assignment for the students would be to graph family sizes for four families they know.

In contrast, some homework is just work that was not completed in school. This kind of homework eases the time constraints of teachers; whatever they don't finish during the day, they assign for homework. But it's not always a good use of our children's time.

Homework can also engage students in higher-order thinking skills. For example, a spelling assignment to use particular words in a paragraph might also specify the paragraph's topic, requiring students to figure out how to use each word in a meaningful way in that given context.

Homework can be a way for teachers to celebrate the diversity of backgrounds in their classes. We've heard about a teacher who asks each student to bring in a favorite family recipe and to find out and write about its origin. Then she collects all of them in a class recipe book. Homework like this validates each child's family and home.

In this quickly changing world, textbooks are often out of date in a year. Homework assignments that direct students to use such resources as the local newspaper can give them much more current information about subjects they are learning. We're fans of weekly current events assignments that ask students to clip and report on newspaper articles about important world or local events. Encourage your child to select articles about events that matter, even if the teacher doesn't specify this. Otherwise you may discover that your children, like ours, pick the shortest articles they can find.

Homework is also a way for teachers to engage parents in what their children are learning in school. We don't mean that a teacher should expect parent and child to do math homework together every night. We mean the kind of homework assignment that might require a child to survey family feelings about such things as an upcoming election or a local debate about building a sewage treatment plant on the south side of town. Homework assignments that ask students to involve their families, friends, and neighbors show them how school and the world outside are interrelated.

Teachers frequently assign research projects that require extra reading and visits to the library. Finding the time for this may not be easy if you work, but we encourage you to put it at the top of your list. Going to the library with your child can be particularly satisfying.

Thoughtful homework assignments motivate students to want to know more about the subject they are working on. Sometimes they also have unintended consequences. One year, for example, third graders at one of our local schools spent all year on a study of the environment, exploring endangered species, pollution, and other related topics. A friend of ours told us that his son really "got it." He became very committed to recycling and was often heard criticizing his parents' habits of throwing things away. "He's right, and we should be doing more recycling," said our friend. "But he's driving us crazy. We're not sure what we can recycle, and we just don't have time to go to the recycling depot." Finally, in desperation, our friend made his son responsible for researching the matter, for collecting and bundling everything properly, and for scheduling trips to the recycling depot. The boy was glad to do it, and the father was, too, once he got used to recycling.

SOME SIDE BENEFITS FOR PARENTS

There are some ways in which homework can be a positive experience for parents.

First of all, it gives you an opportunity to stay in touch with what's happening in school. You can learn from homework what your children are studying and how they are progressing from one topic to another.

You can also get a pretty good picture of how your child is doing by monitoring the homework. We talk more about that in Chapter 6, where we give some suggestions about looking at a child's work as a way of assessing progress.

By reviewing homework, you can get a sense of how interesting and creative the teacher is. You probably won't be very impressed, for example, if your child comes home day after day with nothing but purple ditto sheets.

You can also get ideas about how to enrich your child's education on the weekends and during vacations. When one child we know was studying Spanish, her parents reviewed vocabulary words with her. When she began learning words for food, the whole family went to eat at a Spanish restaurant.

SOME SIDE BENEFITS FOR CHILDREN

In addition to the other reasons for homework, it can also have some unexpected side benefits.

If it is creative, homework can increase your child's interest in school. A neighbor's son was given the assignment to find six different specimens of bugs and bring them to school in jars. An inveterate bug-hater, our friend didn't relish helping him with that assignment! She sent him off alone with jars with holes in the lids, a butterfly net, and her best wishes. He became so interested in his specimens that he asked to go to the library to find a book that would help him identify them—a real first for this kid.

Homework can teach your child responsibility and independence, but you have to provide a little help. If that sounds like a contradiction, it's not. The trick is guiding him without doing it for him. Homework can teach your child how to budget his time and to complete tasks—skills that will be helpful to him all his life.

Homework can actually improve your child's grades. Research shows that in the elementary years, grades are not improved significantly by homework, but in high school, they are, especially by the drill and practice type of homework.

THE ABCs OF HELPING WITH HOMEWORK

GETTING STARTED

• Check with your child nightly to find out if she has homework. For some kids this can be a casual question. For others, who are trying to get away with "forgetting," you might have to be a real nag and ask about each subject separately: "Do you have any math homework?" "Do you have any language arts homework?" Do this for children who need the reminder regardless of their resistance and their age; we know many parents who needed to check with their kids right through high school.

• Buy your child a notebook in which to write assignments.

A colorful notebook, not too small and not too big, will be easy to spot and not too easy to lose. Remember, this is not foolproof! Just because you have purchased the notebook doesn't mean your child will use it.

• Alternatively, you might want to make a weekly grid for your child, with the days of the week across the top and the major subjects (math, language arts, social studies, science) down the left-hand side. Each subject then has a space in which your child can write the daily assignment. This grid can go into a folder or in the front of a three-ring binder.

• Try to be home when your child is doing homework. Your presence in the house might help her focus, especially if you are in the same room. One of us does "homework" from work at the dining room table while her child does homework from school.

SETTING RULES

• Establish very clear homework rules. You won't find either of us ever advocating rigidity in parenting, except where homework rules are concerned. We are strong believers, for example, in a ban on TV during homework time—no exceptions!

• Another important rule is setting a regular time for homework. This will depend on what works best for your child: right after school, after a snack, or later in the evening. No doubt this time will have to be somewhat flexible, but it will help avoid fights if it's understood that a certain time—five o'clock, say—is homework time.

• Some other things to consider when you're making your rules are these: Are telephone calls okay during homework? (We think not.) What about snacks? (Neither of us objects to this.) Is it okay to play background music on the radio?

(This seems all right to us, too.) Who will be around to observe that the rules are kept? (In our families, homework is always done in the evening so that a parent can supervise it.)

• Another consideration: Do you want to establish consequences for incomplete or poorly done homework? We know parents who take away television for the evening or revoke telephone privileges. We've also heard of parents who get their children up very early in the morning to complete homework. To us this seems like punishing the parents.

• If your child is studying or doing a project with a friend, set up some groundrules so that this is beneficial to both children: no TV or telephone, for example. With your careful supervision, you might see your child's self-esteem improve as he explains a difficult concept to his friend. Or perhaps you'll see his quiet partner become assertive and see them organize their work better.

PROVIDING THE BASICS

• Provide a good homework space for your child. With two of our kids, the kitchen or dining room table was best. With the other, who was more self-disciplined, the privacy of her bedroom was preferable. Try to make sure that wherever it is, your child will not have distractions competing for his attention, such as siblings playing or a loud television nearby.

• Keep your child well supplied with everything needed to do the homework: looseleaf paper, construction paper, plain unlined paper, a few sheets of oak tag or poster board, pencils and pens, crayons, magic markers, glue, correction fluid, ruler, and compass or protractor.

• Provide up-to-date reference materials such as a dictionary, thesaurus, atlas, and almanac. Your child's teacher or the local librarian can help you choose the most appropriate for your child's age.

• We don't think it's important to have an encyclopedia in the house since the world is changing so rapidly. If it's at all possible, take your child to the public or school library to use the encyclopedia and other specialized reference materials there.

HELPING OUT

• Be a resource for your child. Check to see that she understands the assignment. If not, go over the directions with her or help her do a few problems. The most important principle is this: Don't do your child's work for her! Answer her questions or help her find the answers for herself, but don't do her work. If she asks you how to spell a word, for example, help her find it in the dictionary.

• When you offer to help, be prepared for conflict. It will happen. "You're not doing it like Mrs. Smith does" or "I always do all the problems, and she doesn't even check them every day." We can almost guarantee that you'll get comments like these. Don't let them discourage you from volunteering to assist.

• Help your child study for a test by reviewing her textbook or notes with her, by scheduling her free time so that it includes time to study, by reviewing concepts after each chapter, and by keeping the evening before and the day of the test as stress free as possible. (Of course, we know that trying to have a stress-free evening is almost guaranteed to fail. That will be the night you have to work late, the dinner burns, and you forget about basketball practice.)

• Don't take over teaching your child. That's not your job. Your methods might contradict the teacher's and might confuse rather than help your child. If he has an assignment he cannot do because the material appears to be new to him, write a note to his teacher. Explain why your son didn't do the assignment and let the teacher know that you did not want to teach the material in case you did it the wrong way.

• Especially, don't offer your child "tricks" for doing math problems. You probably have a way of getting to the answer more quickly than the way she was taught. The teacher, however, is more concerned with the *process* by which your child gets to the answer than with her speed.

SOLVING HOMEWORK PROBLEMS

• If your child forgets to write down his assignment or doesn't understand what to do, encourage him to call a classmate. Or you can call a classmate's parent to check on his or her understanding of what's been assigned. If this is consistently a problem, you might ask the teacher to initial the assignment pad each day to make sure it is correct.

• Know your child's attention span, and schedule breaks accordingly. A simple kitchen timer can help you with this. Let's say your child has forty minutes of homework, but it's hard for her to concentrate for more than fifteen minutes. When she starts her homework, set the timer. When it rings, give her a short break. Maybe she can have an apple or a piece of cheese, or perhaps just a little conversation with you. When the break is over, it's back to work, with the timer on again.

• Your child's after-school activities might become a problem as he gets older and has more and more homework. Even some younger children get overwhelmed by trying to cope with homework and dance class the same night.

• Try not to nag your child when you see her daydreaming or fooling around instead of doing her work. We use the word "try" deliberately because we know how difficult it can be! The more you nag, however, the more she'll hate homework.

• Don't be afraid to point out to a teacher any homework that you find inappropriate. Occasionally, assignments require children to review their family history or survey parents' views on personal, political, or religious issues. Other times, a teacher might ask a child to do a project or take a trip that would cause a financial strain. In either case, you have every right to write a brief, friendly note to the teacher saying that your child did not do the assignment because you felt it was an invasion of privacy or because you could not afford it.

• If you believe the homework is too difficult for your child or is taking too much time, don't hesitate to write the teacher about this. It may well be that this is the first signal of a problem your child is having, or it may simply mean that the teacher doesn't realize she is assigning too much homework.

FOLLOWING UP

• Praise your child's hard work when she's finishing her math assignment, studying her spelling words, or preparing for a social studies test. Acknowledge the difficulty of certain assignments, and praise her persistence.

• Take responsibility for checking that your child has completed his homework and placed it in his bookbag next to the door from which he leaves in the morning. We've struggled through the homework nightmare only to find out that our children left their homework at home! For older children, just ask if the homework is in the bookbag; don't check it yourself.

• Leave time in the morning to double-check the bookbag and to find missing homework. Do this even if you checked it the night before.

• Make sure you ask to see your child's homework after it has been returned by the teacher. Check to see if there are any comments, corrections, or problems with the work. We believe that uncorrected homework is worthless. The mother of a first grader told us recently that after many fights, she decided to let the homework go undone. "I figured, let her pay the consequences," said this mom. "Only guess what? There were no consequences. Susie was right when she told us she didn't have to do the homework."

If your child's homework is not being corrected, either by the teacher or by another child, talk with the teacher about this. If you cannot get her to change her practice, correct the homework yourself. That way your child will be able to learn from his mistakes.

LONG-TERM ASSIGNMENTS

• As we suggested in Chapter 1, keep a calendar on the refrigerator for due dates of long-term assignments such as research papers, dioramas, and book reports.

• When a long-term assignment is given, help your child make a list of the supplies needed and purchase them as soon as possible. This will eliminate those last-minute runs to the discount store to find poster board, popsicle sticks, or construction paper for a project due the following day.

• Help your child sort out what might appear to be an overwhelming homework or project assignment by asking questions such as: What do you think you have to do first? And second? And third? Where do you think you might have to look to find the answer to the problem? In this way, you will provide organizational structure to the task ahead and make it seem less threatening to your child.

• Help your child set up a timeline to complete a long-term assignment. For example, for a book report, set a date for finishing the reading, another for completing the rough draft, a third for finishing the final draft, and finally, one for making the cover. Then help her devise a work schedule—perhaps fifteen minutes a night until the project is done. This way she can review and revise her work, and you both avoid the stress of doing it all at 9:30 the night before it's due.

• Talk about the topic of a long-term assignment while he's working on it. At dinner or in the car, encourage him to share what he has learned. A few conversations like this can help the subject come alive.

• Offer to help proofread the final paper. Point out where corrections need to be made, perhaps with check marks penciled in the margins, but don't make them yourself. This will help your child put her best foot forward by turning in a corrected and good-looking paper.

THE FINAL WORD

At this point maybe you're thinking that we've made a big fuss about nothing. Your children do their homework rather routinely, they don't ask for your help, and while they don't love it, they don't think of homework as something worse than taking medicine. You're lucky! You're also an exception to the rule.

"I didn't understand why there was all the hullaballoo about homework until Sally was in the sixth grade and had so much trouble with math," said a friend of ours, who then had to take a crash course in homework-helping techniques. To those of you who are already having a tough time with homework, our advice will not make the tensions and dilemmas disappear. We do hope, though, that our suggestions will help minimize the difficulties. "Although it's painful to set limits, the only thing that gets us through homework every day is the fact that we have routines and clear expectations," one mother reported to us.

You'll notice that all of our suggestions require your involvement. This often means you have to make choices —perhaps between attending the PTA meeting that has an interesting speaker or staying home to supervise completion of the book report due the next day. A working mom told us, "I leave work at five o'clock each evening so that I can get home to supervise homework. Sometimes that means I have to take work home. That's the choice I make."

Perhaps you'll have to make that choice only when your child is in fourth grade, or perhaps you will face the dilemma for many years. In either case, we guarantee that you will, like countless other parents before you, survive homework!

6

HOW IS YOUR CHILD DOING?

We all want to know how our children are doing in school. In this chapter, we take a look at some of the ways we can find answers to this question, and we also point out some of the signs that indicate your child might be having a problem. Finally, we suggest what you can do when the answers you find aren't the ones you wanted to find.

While report cards and standardized test scores are the official way we learn how our children are doing in school, there are many other richer and more immediate ways to assess our children's learning. As parents, we are always observing our children, but we may be unaware that we are actually assessing them.

One mother pointed out, "It took a problem with my son and the helpful advice of a friend with an older child before I realized that taking stock of my child's academic health was similar to taking stock of his physical health." The process was basically the same: She observed her son, gathered as many facts as she could, asked him a bunch of questions, organized her findings into a coherent list, and then spoke to an expert (who can be a doctor or the teacher). And just like physical symptoms, academic ills are sometimes hidden and difficult to uncover. We hope our suggestions in this chapter will help you begin to assess your child's progress yourself.

With this kind of knowledge, based on firsthand evidence, you can better judge the accuracy of standardized tests, report cards, and teacher comments. You can also be a better audience and advocate for your child when you know her strengths and weaknesses well.

WHAT WE CAN SEE FOR OURSELVES

The daily work of our children, at home and in class, can tell us quickly and concretely whether or not they're learning what is taught. Especially in the early grades, it's easy to observe how our children are doing. To figure out how well they are reading, for example, we can ask them to read a story (or even a page) aloud. We try to use a book from school so that we can judge how well they're doing on grade-level material. We watch and listen to see if they stumble over a lot of the words or stop often to sound them out. We observe whether they are reading smoothly and fluently, and usually we ask a couple of questions about the material to see if they understand what they are reading.

You might want to know if your child is mastering other skills that you know are being taught. For example, if he has been learning to read maps, you might ask him to help you find several locations on a map of your town. Or maybe you can make up some simple word problems using the math concepts you saw him working on for homework.

We find that it is important to be casual about our detective work. If we make a big deal of it, our children will resist us and perhaps refuse to demonstrate what they know. We also might make them anxious or lead them to think we believe something is wrong.

We want to emphasize that you can trust the evidence of your own eyes and ears about schoolwork. When you hear your child read well, that means she is reading well. You can observe for yourself whether she can tell time or make change, too. And if she can't, and you continue to watch her carefully, you might even be able to figure out what the difficulty is.

We do have to be careful to keep everything in its proper perspective, however, as this mother learned.

> When Elaine was in third grade, I asked her to read me a story from a schoolbook she had in her bookbag. I wasn't worried about her—that is, until she started to read the story.
>
> Elaine had a tremendous amount of trouble pronouncing the words in the story, and the cadence of her reading was choppy. I stopped her after a couple of pages. By then it was obvious that she was frustrated and had no idea what she had read. I was a basket case.
>
> "How could this be?" I asked myself. Elaine had just read me a story the week before, and although her reading hadn't been perfect, it hadn't been this flawed. I was sick with worry and called my friend whose son was in Elaine's class. She said she hadn't seen the book and suggested I speak to the teacher the next day.

When she called the teacher, Elaine's mom found out that she had worried unnecessarily. The book Elaine had brought home was to be read in April or May (it was then October), and the teacher said she wasn't surprised that Elaine wasn't ready for it.

It gets more difficult to stay on top of things when our

children reach middle school and high school. The work gets harder and the subject matter more specialized. Although we may not know where they are with trigonometry, however, we can still tell how long it takes them to do their homework, and we can observe them to see how confident they are about their work. When they get older, we have to be especially careful about our questions. Adolescents don't tolerate their parents' interference as well as young children.

By observation we sometimes find that our children are doing much better than their grades or tests would lead us to believe. Other times we can see a problem long before it shows up on a test. Here are two school-related areas to which we parents need to pay particular attention.

ATTITUDES TOWARD SCHOOL

The ten-year-old son of one of our friends didn't want to go to school. Randy got a stomachache every morning just when it was time to leave for the bus, and he didn't talk about school eagerly and happily as his older brother did. Every time the subject was raised, he clammed up. This behavior indicated to our friend that Randy might not be doing well in school.

When children feel valued, competent, and comfortable in school—something we can tell from the way they talk about their classmates, schoolwork, and the teacher—then most likely they are doing all right. When a child feels unhappy, angry, or incompetent, however, a problem might be impeding progress, and we need to step in.

The best way to start is by asking lots of questions, casually, and when appropriate. We don't want to put our children through the third degree; we just want to see if we can pinpoint where the problem is.

The first thing we want to investigate is probably the child's perception of himself in relation to his schoolwork. The questions that follow explore this:

- What is your favorite subject in school?
- What do you like about it?
- Do you think you do well in it?
- What subject don't you like so much?
- What don't you like about it?
- Could I help you with it? Could the teacher?

Sometimes a child's progress in school is slowed by a poor relationship with a teacher. Many children are open about their dislike of a teacher; others are subtly devalued by the teacher and consequently do poorly in school without being aware of the reason. You can learn a little concerning your child's feelings about his teacher with questions like these:

- What do you think your teacher likes best about you?
- What did she say about your book report (or spelling test or project—something your child was particularly proud of)?
- What does she do when you do a really good job on something?
- Does your teacher ever get angry with you? For what?
- How do you know when she's angry?
- Does she laugh with you sometimes, too?

Other times, children's problems are not at all related to schoolwork but rather to their relationships with their peers. Occasionally, children have trouble making and keeping friends in school even if they have friends in their neighborhood. Questions like the following might help to uncover trouble in this area:

- Who is your best friend in class?
- Whom do you play with during recess? What do you play?
- Who is your reading partner?
- Whom do you sit next to?
- Whom do you eat lunch with?

We've learned to be careful about interpreting what our children say about school, however. Your son might say, "The teacher is mean," when what is bothering him is that he is finding it difficult to sit still all day—and she is the one reminding him to settle down. He might say, "The other kids don't like me," when he means, "They can read better than I can."

After talking with your child, try to have a conversation with another parent or two from the class, people you can trust not to gossip. This lets you find out whether other children are having similar difficulties.

Then, ready with notes about your concerns, make an appointment with the teacher. (See our suggestions for that meeting in Chapter 3.) Make this appointment even when you're just a *little* worried about your children's attitudes toward school and regardless of their ages. A negative attitude probably means something is wrong.

HOMEWORK

At open school night in the fall, teachers usually let us know their homework expectations: how much homework they give, in what subject areas, and how long it should take.

Sometimes this doesn't fit with what's happening at home. Maybe your daughter is spending an hour on work that her classmates are completing in fifteen minutes. Maybe she's breezing through the work each night. Or perhaps you've observed that she's having a hard time night after night with her math homework.

One mother told this story:

> One night Julie ended up in desperate tears over her homework. Her class had just started subtraction, and she couldn't do the practice problems. She knew what she didn't understand: She couldn't figure out which number was being taken away from which. The more I tried to explain, the more she cried.
>
> Finally, I said, "Just leave it. I'll write a note to Mrs. Rogers. She'll explain this, and you can do the homework tomorrow." That satisfied her, and we put the paper away. I wrote a note, then read it to Julie.
>
> Two days later Mrs. Rogers called me to say, "Thank you." She told me that almost all the children had had trouble with that homework assignment. She just hadn't explained subtraction well enough, she said, but only Julie and I were able to tell her where the misunderstanding was. So our note helped the whole class!

We've often found that a note to the teacher is enough to solve a homework problem. Like Julie's mom, we let our kids read (and approve) the note before we send it, and we try to be as specific as possible about what we have observed.

Sometimes that won't be enough, and it will be necessary for you to meet with the teacher face-to-face. (See our advice in Chapter 3 on preparing for conferences.)

HOW THE SCHOOL REPORTS TO US

The school lets us know in many ways, both formally and informally, how our children are doing. Every time we're asked to sign homework or a test, every time we get a note or speak to the teacher, even in passing, we get information that can help us assess our children's learning.

CLASS TESTS AND WORK

The teacher lets us know almost every week how our children are doing in the classroom. Sometimes this is an obvious sign, such as a test grade; sometimes it's more subtle, such as comments or questions on a homework paper. We need to be on the lookout for all the clues if we want to know how our children are doing.

We have found that cleaning out the bookbag once a week and leafing through the notebook are good ways to keep up. While this may seem like an invasion of your child's privacy, we don't believe it is, especially when she's young. When she's older—perhaps in sixth or seventh grade—we think that unless the child gives you permission (which she probably won't), you probably shouldn't intrude.

Some things you'll want to look for:

Homework. Are there comments or corrections? How extensive are they? Is most of the work acceptable? How do the comments compare with the amount of effort expended? If your child spent an hour on an assignment and it's mostly wrong, she probably needs some extra help. On the other hand, if her work is mostly right, then that just means she needs time to complete her work in that area.

Class Tests. Your children may ask you to help them prepare for the spelling tests on Fridays and the math quizzes on Tuesdays. If they don't, it's perfectly okay to offer them your help. They may not take it, and that's all right, too. Laurette's kids got into college without being drilled on their spelling words or times tables in third grade.

In any case, check on their test grades. Ask yourself: Do I see the results of all the studying? Is my child doing all right in these subjects? Is there a pattern to his mistakes? Is he getting a chance to show what I *know* he knows?

Projects and Book Reports. While class tests can tell us whether our children are mastering the material, projects and book reports give us a broader picture. Is your child meeting the teacher's expectations? Are these expectations clearly defined? How well does your child work independently? How motivated and interested is he in the subject?

REPORT CARDS

The most formal and regular way the school communicates about our children's progress is the report card. Report cards are usually sent home with the children; sometimes they're mailed. Some schools insist that parents show up at the school to get them. In elementary school we are usually asked to sign and return them to show we've looked them over.

By the way, noncustodial parents have the right to have report cards and all other mailings, flyers, and special notices sent to them, in addition to the copies sent to custodial parents. While this sounds easy, it is not so simple for the school. In fact, your request for duplicate mailings may end up falling through the cracks. Just keep reminding the school each time you discover that has happened. By keeping on top of this, you will be helping other noncustodial parents, too.

While the purpose of report cards hasn't changed over the years, their style and look have changed dramatically. When we were children, our report cards had about a dozen areas (mostly academic subjects and "effort") marked with grades of *A* through *F*. Now report cards are *much* longer. In our school district, the elementary school report card lists more than eighty areas to which grades of 1 to 5 are given; 1 is equivalent to *A* and 5 to *F*—and the children figure this out immediately! A close look reveals that these cover the same basic subjects as before but in much greater detail. For example, what used to be language arts is now reading, oral language, and written language, each with several subcategories, all graded. So instead of a single grade for language arts, in our school system an elementary school child receives a total of nineteen grades (plus three grades for effort). These can be very confusing to sort out. If you're not sure what each grade covers, ask the teacher to explain them to you and your child.

The point of the report card is to let us know how our children have done, both academically and socially. It should also give a youngster credit for effort in each subject. We believe his effort is as important as his accomplishments. Not all children are *A* students; a *B* in math might be the best your child can do. If that's the case, then he should get an *A* for effort to motivate and encourage him to continue to work hard.

We have found that report card time provides a good opportunity for us to talk with our children calmly and candidly about school. The nature of these conversations depends on whether the report you receive from the teacher is positive or negative or somewhere in between. Before you talk to your child, review the card thoroughly. Look for areas where your child has improved from one marking period to the next and for those areas where achievement has declined. Look as well for discrepancies between what the teacher is reporting and what you think you know about your child's performance based on tests you've seen, homework you've signed, and conversations you've had with your child or his teacher.

Try to start these talks with your child on a positive note even when you are disturbed by the report card. Occasionally, it won't be easy to find something to compliment.

> Bill, when I looked at your report card, I noticed that you improved your effort grade in both math and science. I bet you feel good that all your hard work paid off. Mr. Smith gave you a better mark because of it. Good job!

Next, try to learn how your child perceives the grades on the card. You might say something like this:

> Barbara, I have some thoughts about your report card. But before I tell you what I think, I would be interested in hearing whether you think you got the marks you deserved. Did you expect most of the grades you received, or did they surprise you?

Usually, kids are right on target. They know how well they're doing, what they need help in, what their "good" subjects are, and what the "bad" ones are, too. They also have a good sense of what's fair. So if your child says that his grade in social studies isn't "fair" and his story corroborates what you've seen in his tests and the work he's done at home, then you should make an appointment to talk to his teacher.

Try to find out if your child has any ideas about how she can improve her grade in a particular subject.

Felicia, your teacher has written a note on the report card saying that you need to work harder in language arts. Do you think he's right? Why don't we try to think of things you can do. Do you have any ideas?

There have been times when, despite what our children told us about how hard they worked, we knew they didn't put much effort into their work. In those cases, we challenged them to do better.

THE PERMANENT RECORD

In 1974, our right to review our children's permanent records and to challenge any unfair or inaccurate comments in them was legislated by the Freedom of Information Act, which is part of the federal Family Educational Rights and Privacy Act. This act also prohibits the school from releasing student records to other agencies or institutions without our permission.

A permanent record card is started when a child enters kindergarten and follows him until he graduates from high school. If he leaves the school district, a copy is usually sent to his new school. The card contains such things as end-of-the-year grades, attendance and health records, standardized test scores, reports and recommendations to staff from school support personnel, honors and special recognitions, and disciplinary actions.

We think it's a good idea to try to review our children's permanent record cards every few years. One thing to look for is descriptive information recorded on the card that is clearly an invasion of your family's privacy—"Jan's mom is an alcoholic," for example. You might also look for information that is inaccurate or irrelevant—"José's parents are extremely rich and live in a fancy house." We look, too, for harmful information or words that label our children—"Tom never sits still" or "Liz is antisocial."

The school secretary will arrange an appointment for you to review the permanent record card. Parents are not allowed to do this alone; by law, the principal or her designee must sit with you to make sure you don't tamper with anything.

Each school district has a policy specifying what to do when a parent wants something changed or removed from the permanent record. We've never asked to have anything changed, but a principal we know told us about a parent who did. The parent felt that what the teacher had written—"Greg is a sneaky boy"—would predispose a new teacher to look at her child negatively. The principal checked with the teacher to find out why she had written that statement and agreed that the phrase should be deleted from the card. The comment was removed and replaced with the statement: "Greg doesn't always work alone and sometimes looks to his friends for help."

If the principal will not agree to remove something objectionable from the record, you can appeal the decision to the superintendent. We don't know anyone who has challenged the information on the permanent record, but we do know many parents who review it regularly, especially when their children are moving to a new school.

STANDARDIZED TESTS

Almost no aspect of education gets more attention than standardized tests. Not only do the scores get wide publicity, but they are used to make many high-stakes decisions. Schools are sometimes judged good or bad based on their scores and whether they have gone up or down. Many students spend a lot of time in class practicing to take the tests and then are placed in groups or special programs based on their scores. Sometimes students are tested before they even enter kindergarten, supposedly to determine whether or not they're ready for school.

A test is *standardized* if it is given to a large number of people under roughly the same conditions. Most school systems give standardized tests every year beginning in the second grade to measure students' achievement in reading and math. Some of the most commonly used tests are the California Achievement Test (CAT), the Iowa Test of Basic Skills (ITBS), and the Metropolitan Achievement Test (MAT). These tests appear to us to be more similar than different, although test publishers and experts like to emphasize their differences. (Test publishing has become very big business in the United States.)

Many states mandate statewide tests in addition to the basic skills tests chosen by the district. Some of these are given every year, while others are given only at certain grade levels in order to assess student progress in such areas as writing, science, or math at what are thought to be critical points in the school career (fourth and eighth grades, for example).

Test Scores: What Do They Mean?

In order to interpret test scores, first you need to know what kind of test you're looking at. Most standardized tests given to our children in school are *norm-referenced*; that is, they compare each child's score to a norm or the scores of other children of the same age who have already taken the test. The comparison is usually expressed in a percentile score. A child scoring at the eightieth percentile, for example, had more correct answers than eighty percent of other children on her grade level; twenty percent of them had more correct answers than she did.

Norm-referenced tests are based on the assumption that scores should fall along a bell-shaped or normal curve. Norm-referenced tests give a small number of students very high or very low scores; most students fall in the center. Critics of standardized tests question this practice, pointing out that the distribution of human abilities and knowledge doesn't necessarily fall along a bell-shaped curve.

In contrast, almost everyone who takes a *criterion-referenced* test could, in theory at least, pass it. The written test we take to get a driver's license is an example. Our scores are not compared with others. The test simply measures whether or not we've mastered the material, and our scores reflect our correct answers. Chances are that most of the class spelling and math tests your child takes in elementary school are criterion-referenced.

WHAT TESTS *CAN* TELL US

Remember filling in little circles on answer sheets with number-two pencils? Well, the tests today are virtually the same, right down to the pencils. They're usually multiple choice in format. This means they're really testing the ability to recognize (or guess at) correct answers, not the ability to solve problems, say those who oppose standardized tests.

This is probably true, but standardized tests are efficient. They're easy to score, and they provide ways to compare populations of students across schools, cities, and even states. Standardized tests allow us to look at how fifth graders in New Jersey are doing compared to fifth graders in

California. State legislators and governors like to have this kind of information, as do parents moving into a school district. They believe that through test scores schools are held accountable for children's learning and that higher scores mean better schools. That may sound logical, but it doesn't work that way. First of all, we can only compare schools with virtually identical populations. Even then we're not really getting an accurate picture of children's learning since most standardized tests discriminate against poor, minority, and female children. Furthermore, unless we're interested in looking at test-taking skills, most standardized tests don't tell us very much about how our sons and daughters are doing at the things we care about: reading, writing, arithmetic, and *thinking*.

What Tests *Cannot* Tell Us

A standardized test, at best, measures performance on a particular day with a particular set of questions within a prescribed time limit. It doesn't tell us how a child synthesizes information, thinks through alternatives, or solves problems—skills that are probably much more important to the child's future success than the discrete items measured in multiple-choice questions. In fact, there is growing evidence that standardized tests actually penalize creative or diverse thinkers who are able to see more than one right answer. Some parents and educators even question whether standardized tests measure what they claim; reading and understanding a book are quite different from reading a paragraph and answering multiple-choice questions about it, for example.

THE TESTING DILEMMA

When the reading scores of a friend's daughter declined quite a bit several years ago, her mother was very worried. She was also confused because it seemed to her that Erica was reading very well. When she and the teacher examined the breakdown of scores, it turned out that Erica's mistakes were mostly in the section where she had to answer questions about specific passages. The teacher suggested that because the passages were quite boring and were printed in small, hard-to-read type, Erica probably just didn't want to bother reading them again to answer the questions.

Although it can be hard, we parents have to try to keep standardized testing in perspective. Erica's mother found out that her daughter's lower scores were probably the result of a lack of persistence—not poor achievement. They were not a good indicator of how well Erica was reading.

The dilemma Erica's mother faced was what to do about the test scores. She knew that Erica's scores mattered. They would be used to place her in a reading group and to determine her eligibility for the school's gifted and talented program. She also knew that the score was an inaccurate measure of Erica's reading achievement and didn't measure the skills and abilities her mother believed in and had tried to nurture in her daughter: creativity, problem solving, and critical thinking.

When a parent believes that a child's scores are not accurate, he or she can request that the test be given again. If there's a good reason, the district will usually comply with the request. In our opinion, however, there is almost no reason good enough to justify putting a child through the tests a second time and perhaps giving the message that the child has failed or has serious problems. You might want to consider making the request, however, if you're very concerned about your child's scores because the discrepancy is quite large or because you think he belongs in advanced math and a low score might prevent that placement.

A better alternative would be to make an appointment with the district's testing coordinator or someone else with expertise in testing. The two of you can go over those sections of the test about which you're concerned and analyze your child's specific mistakes item by item. You might discover a pattern to the mistakes, or you might find something as simple as a circle skipped on the answer sheet. In either case, you will then be able to attach a note to the test report explaining the scores.

In Erica's case, her mother and teacher decided that the low scores wouldn't really hurt her that year, and they agreed to work together to help her understand the importance of doing her best the following year.

TEST-TAKING ATTITUDES AND SKILLS

Some children take tests without much anxiety, others get a little nervous, and some get very nervous. It's not hard to know where your child fits in this spectrum, but it is difficult to tell how much of this comes from the child, how much from you, and how much from the environment. The trick is finding the right balance. On the one hand, we don't want to tell our children that tests don't matter at all; in reality, they do. On the other hand, we don't want to create too much pressure by overemphasizing tests.

Testing experts suggest that we give our children the dual message that they should do the best they can but that they should also understand this is just one test on one day. It will not define once and for all who they are or what they can or cannot do.

What can we do if our children get all worked up about tests? Well, first figure out why there's a problem. The teacher might be able to add something to what our children tell us and what we observe. It might be that one boy has trouble following the directions, another finds it hard to make the marks in the little circles on the answer sheet, and still another worries about the time limit. In these cases, they may just need to do some practice tests to feel more comfortable. The teacher can tell you if the class will be doing this. If not, he might be able to send home some practice tests.

Some children get anxious or feel incompetent when they take standardized tests because the questions are out of context and appear to be unrelated to what they're learning in school. Other children get anxious because they're competitive. We heard about one child who gets violently ill the morning of standardized testing; if she is forced to go to school, she throws up when she gets there. Then she has to go home and take the test another day, at a special makeup time. For children like these, you'll want to downplay the importance of the test. It's necessary, though, to acknowledge their anxiety. Instead of telling them not to worry or that the test isn't important, we think it is more helpful to say something like this: "I know you're nervous, and I know how important it is to you to do well on this test. You will! And remember: You'll have lots of other chances to show what you can do. Just do your best." And then change the subject.

AN ALTERNATIVE TO STANDARDIZED TESTING: PERFORMANCE-BASED ASSESSMENT

The good news is that among educators and parents there is a growing movement away from standardized tests and toward what is variously called *alternative*, *authentic*, or *performance-based* assessment. This kind of assessment uses a variety of things, often put together in a *portfolio*, to evaluate a child's learning. For example, writing samples, classroom tests, writing and reading logs, written observations, and anecdotes can all find their way into the portfolio. The examples of student work usually include some of what both the student and teacher consider the student's very best efforts. Sometimes records of performances or exhibitions are also included. The wonderful thing about a portfolio is that it gives a well-rounded picture of what a student is actually learning and achieving over time; it shows actual student progress.

The state social studies test might ask questions about things your son hasn't yet encountered, but this is unlikely to happen in a teacher-designed classroom test. Instead of grading him on short-answer questions about the rain forest, say advocates of alternative assessment, why not grade him based on a performance—a classroom debate—where he gets to show off everything he's learned?

Assessment like this has not yet found its way formally into most schools, and it's unlikely you'll persuade your school system to institute alternative assessment techniques overnight. If you're interested in getting schoolpeople and parents talking about these ideas, however, bring it up with the school principal and the PTA. Maybe the PTA could sponsor a forum on assessment for one of its meetings.

Maybe the principal has some ideas about a good speaker or other resources. Maybe she even has some suggestions about things you could do.

Performance-based assessment is not an esoteric idea, however. It is what parents and teachers already do in order to figure out how well children are progressing. We recommend throughout this book that you look closely at your child's work; that's parental performance-based assessment. You could certainly create your own small portfolio of your child's homework, test papers, and projects to take with you to the parent-teacher conference to give both you and the teacher concrete examples to look at while you talk. And the typical folder of work waiting for you on open school night is a small portfolio, even if the teacher doesn't call it that.

GROUPING AND PLACEMENTS

Another important source of information is *grouping*—the ways in which our children's classes are organized for instruction. This can tell us a lot about how our children are doing compared to their classmates and about the teacher's instructional methods.

HETEROGENEOUS VERSUS HOMOGENEOUS GROUPING

Essentially, there are two ways to form groups: *homogeneously* (putting together students of roughly the same achievement level) and *heterogeneously* (mixing achievement levels). Some people mistakenly think of homogeneous groups as being formed on the basis of ability. This is not true. They're usually formed on the basis of factors such

as standardized test scores, grades, and teacher recommendations—all of which look at achievement, not innate
ability.

Tracking is an extreme version of homogeneous grouping: the formation of whole classes by achievement level.
It's very common in middle schools and high schools, and,
although less common in elementary schools, it does exist
in some.

Both homogeneous and heterogeneous groups have their
places, in our opinion. The typical elementary school reading and math groups, for example, are homogeneous
groups. When students are learning new skills that require
previous mastery of other skills—as is the case in reading
and math—it makes sense to group students who are working at roughly the same level. Otherwise, it doesn't.

Think about learning to swim. Beginning, intermediate,
and advanced groups need to work separately when learning new skills. Beginning students might be learning arm
movements while intermediate students are refining their
breathing skills and advanced students are learning to turn.
Each would be excluded a good deal of the time—and
bored!—if they were all in the same instructional group.
Put the same students in a gymnastics class, and you would
probably have to form entirely different groups since swimming expertise doesn't equal gymnastics expertise.

What sounds logical for swimming and gymnastics is the
subject of heated debates in schools. Tracked classes are
based on the assumption that students who are good readers
will also excel at all other subjects, with the reverse also
being true. But that turns out not to be the case.

Educators and parents who support tracking also believe
that children learn better with others who have similar
achievement levels. With the specific exception we noted,
there is no research evidence to support this belief at the

elementary school level. While research results are more mixed at the secondary level, recent studies do not demonstrate compelling evidence of tracking's benefits for any students. Quite the opposite. Research demonstrates the negative effects of tracking on low-track students: low self-esteem, low expectations, and a progressively wider gap between their skills and knowledge and those of high-track students. All too often, children who are placed in low tracks in the early grades remain there for the rest of their school careers.

FLEXIBLE GROUPING

The best approach seems to be what is called *flexible grouping*—the use of different kinds of groups for different activities and purposes. In a classroom using flexible grouping, no groups are permanent, and children belong to many different groups. If you spent a day in such a classroom, you'd probably become a proponent of flexible grouping, too. During the course of the day you might see the twenty-five third graders in several different configurations. Perhaps language arts might start the morning. In three or four homogeneous groups, children might be reading from a book and discussing what they're reading. Then the teacher may ask them to form smaller groups of three or four children—heterogeneous groups put together to write scripts for skits they will perform for one another. Later in the day, after the children return from art class, the teacher may put them in a third group to start a research project in math. Unlike the others, these groups might be formed randomly. Twice in the afternoon, children may be in still different groups—once with a partner to do a science experiment, perhaps, and once with a small social studies

group studying for the chapter test. One teacher who works
this way told us:

> It's not easy to regroup children so many times during
> the day, but I can't think of teaching any other way. I wish
> I had known about it fifteen years ago when I started teach-
> ing. Although it's harder for me, I believe it capitalizes on
> the best in each child. It breaks down the assumption that
> because a student is good in reading or math, he's great in
> everything.

Children in this kind of classroom learn to appreciate
each other's talents and contributions. They also learn to
work with others who have diverse backgrounds and
abilities—as they will have to in the future in most work-
places. Parents can see the results of this for themselves:

> In his fourth-grade class, my son's teacher grouped chil-
> dren differently for each subject. I remember how surprised
> and happy Rick was when his buddy from the Recreation
> Department day camp was placed in the same group as he
> was. "Mom, Jon is in my social studies group," he told me
> excitedly. "And boy, is he smart!"
> He went on to tell me that Jon had always been in a
> reading group with children who were slower. He said he
> had thought that Jon wasn't very smart. "He says his step-
> father watches the news with him every night and that they
> talk about it afterward. He knows much more about current
> events than I do. Do you think we could watch the news
> together tonight?"

This nine-year-old's view of his friend changed dramatically
in just one day. And we can imagine that Jon also felt more
competent than he ever had before because of how the
teacher placed him.

Questions for the Teacher

The way a teacher groups children has a great impact on children's self-esteem. So ask your child's teachers a lot of questions about their grouping philosophy and practices:

- What groups is my daughter in?
- How did you decide upon the groups?
- Is there flexibility to move between groups? What will you do if my daughter's skills get better? How will you know if her skills change?
- Does my daughter get the chance to work with other children who have different achievement levels?
- If my daughter is in a low reading or math group, what are her chances of moving to a higher group? Is she being exposed to the same content as children in higher groups?
- Is she being challenged? Is she learning to solve problems and think critically?

We ask these questions as much to influence the teacher's thinking as to find out about her grouping philosophy. Don't expect to turn an advocate of tracking into a proponent of flexible grouping in a meeting or two. It is possible to influence the way the teacher sees your child, however, and increase the opportunities available to her. Over time, opening up more opportunities to children, one by one, is a major accomplishment!

Further Reading

Ginger E. Black. *Making the Grade: How to Help Your Child Have a Happy and Successful School Experience.* New York: Lyle Stuart, 1989.

Ann Boehm and Mary Alice White. *The Parents' Handbook*

on School Testing. New York: Teachers College Press, 1982.

Dorothy Corkville Briggs. *Your Child's Self-Esteem*. New York: Doubleday Dolphin Books, 1975.

Adele Faber and Elaine Mazlish. *How to Talk So Kids Will Listen and Listen So Kids Will Talk*. New York: Avon Books, 1980.

National Center for Citizens in Education. *Parents CAN Understand Testing*. Columbia, MD: 1980.

National Center for Fair and Open Testing (Fairtest). *Standardized Tests and Our Children: A Guide to Testing Reform*. Cambridge, MA: 1990.

Jeannie Oakes. *Keeping Track: How Schools Structure Inequality*. New Haven, CT: Yale University Press, 1985.

7

ROADBLOCKS TO LEARNING

Our children's problems in school don't always present themselves in bold and dramatic ways. Sometimes we know something isn't quite right, but we're not sure what the problem is. We have to look for the causes of problems that we can't quite define.

We might think that our children are just not performing up to their capabilities, based on past performance in school, test scores, and achievements in other areas. It might seem that they're not doing as well as we think they should be doing; they're not very interested in schoolwork, study as little as possible, and give up easily. Both parents and teachers are frustrated by this, wondering why children don't do what they're capable of doing. Often they're seen as lazy children when other forces are usually at work. Before you start pushing, though—a natural reaction!— try to take a clear look at your child's achievement and decide whether or not she's doing her best.

Start by talking with your child; this gives you the best clues. While you don't need to do it every night, do ask your child fairly often to "tell you the story of his days." What you should listen for are stories or offhand remarks that suggest something is not quite right.

In addition, review all the sources of information described in Chapter 6—reports from teachers, report cards, homework, tests sent home for signing, and the like.

To most of us, our own children are bright and interesting—and of course they are!—but that doesn't mean they should or can get straight As in every subject. Here are some things to consider when grappling with this issue:

- Look at what your child enjoys doing and feels competent at, especially the attention, care, and standards to which she holds herself in that activity. If she enjoys playing the piano, for example, how often and for how long does she practice? How does she react when she makes a mistake? When is she satisfied with the quality of her playing? How does that compare with the way she does her schoolwork?
- Listen to what your child says about himself in comparison with other children in the class. Does he feel competent compared with most of them? Does he believe that he's in the right reading group, for example? How satisfied is he with his progress?
- Ask your child what she thinks: Does she believe that she's doing her best? In what areas does she think she could do better? How does she think you could help her?

This issue is not an easy one to resolve. We don't want to create either overachievers or underachievers. As parents, we must demand that our children do their best and hold appropriately high standards for themselves, but we must not pressure them so much that we take the fun out of learning. Pushing our children to always be the best will ultimately be counterproductive, we believe. But we don't want to ignore what looks like persistent underachievement, either. If that's really what is going on, then the next step is to figure out *why* in order to do something about it.

WARNING SIGNS

There are some clear warning signs of problems. We've separated them into categories related to a child's physical, social, emotional, and academic or cognitive growth or development. This is an artificial separation, however, since these areas are interrelated. Lack of success or development in one area can definitely influence another. Unfortunately, schools do not always recognize *all* parts of a child's development; they tend to look only at a child's academic progress and ignore the other areas. It is important for us as parents, therefore, to be particularly aware of the interrelationships.

While we do not discount the multitude of books that give benchmarks or guidelines for what our children should be doing cognitively, emotionally, socially, and physically at various ages, we do caution you about taking these guidelines too seriously. They are nothing more than lists based on research of what a typical ten-year-old or a typical five-year-old can do. How many typical kids are there? Not many whose profiles would *exactly* fit those given by the guidebooks, we'd bet.

We suggest that you consider the lists as very rough guides and not as exact rules of child development. We haven't reproduced them here because they are easily accessible to you. We've listed a few books at the end of the chapter, and the local librarian can direct you to others. And you can use your child's friends as more useful guides to what is typical of each age. Use your observation powers and some of the following questions to see if you need to take a closer look.

PHYSICAL DEVELOPMENT

• Does your child complain frequently about going to school?

• Are stomach cramps and a sore throat a typical part of the morning scene?

• Does your child find it hard to sit still? At home does she wiggle around all the time—is her "motor going" constantly? Does the teacher tell you the same story?

• Does your child often appear tired? Does he have trouble going to sleep at night?

• Do you see a change in your child's eating habits or appetite? Is she suddenly eating a lot less or a lot more? Is she suddenly not interested or very interested in food?

• Does your child seem to have difficulty with fine motor skills (holding and writing with a pencil, for example)? Or with gross motor skills (running, riding a bicycle, and so forth)?

SOCIAL DEVELOPMENT

• Does your child complain about being lonely?

• Does she have any friends in her class, the school, or the neighborhood?

• If she doesn't, does she say or act as though it bothers her? Does she talk about it? Does she tell you why she has no friends?

• If she has friends, does she fight with them a lot? Does the teacher tell you the same thing happens in school?

• Does she talk too much in school—and get in trouble for it? What does she say is the reason that she talks so much?

• How does your child interact with siblings? With other family members?

Emotional Development

• Does your child seem anxious or depressed about school or his life in general? (Depression in children can manifest itself in many ways—perhaps a sad face all the time, poor appetite, frequent crying or sighing, or withdrawal.)
• Has your child suddenly become argumentative or rude—with his family and in school, too?
• Is he nonresponsive to questions about school? Or does he burst into tears when it is mentioned?
• Does your child seem to be overly dependent on you? Does he have difficulty separating from you? Does he depend on you to get started with his homework?
• Does your child approach new situations with a great deal of fear or anxiety? Is he so afraid that he won't try new experiences?

Academic or Cognitive Development

• Have you noticed a sudden drop in your child's grades in one or more subject areas?
• Are the grades lower than what you believe they should be?
• Does your child have persistent difficulty in one area so that she is falling behind her classmates?
• What is your child's attitude about schoolwork? Does she appear overwhelmed by it? Anxious? Unmotivated? Does she give up without trying when it's difficult?
• Does your child seem very disorganized? Does she leave books and materials in school or at home? Does she lose things often? Is she confused about what's expected of her?

It would be nice if we could now say that if you answered yes to more than two or three questions in each category, you need to do such and such. But it's not that easy.

An affirmative response to some of the questions we posed can mean a number of things. Here comes the need for more detective work and for *communication* with the school; we can't emphasize enough how important communication is. Teachers, principals, and school support staff have a great deal of experience—they have probably seen hundreds of children in their careers—and can prove invaluable as you seek to discover if there is a problem and decide what to do about it. Talk with them.

In this chapter, we explore with you what affirmative answers to some of our questions might mean. Maybe the problem is not a school problem after all but is related instead to something at home. It might also be that your child is doing too much, which is not so unusual in today's overscheduled world. Another common explanation is, quite simply, immaturity. It could also be that your child is having difficulties in school because she's not challenged enough. We also discuss learning and thinking styles and how a mismatch between your child's style and the school's might cause problems.

ARE THERE PROBLEMS AT HOME?

One possible reason for difficulties at school might be your child's preoccupation with problems at home. When families experience major upheavals such as divorce, remarriage, death, a move, or a new child, the impact on children is usually clear. We've learned, however, that other things happening at home might also affect children in school. Children hear everything, and what they don't hear, they intuit. Conversations about money problems or the critical illness of a loved one (even a person who doesn't live in the house) might cause a child to have problems, and so might a parent's new job or new work schedule.

Because children internalize so much, we might not be aware of how much anxiety and stress these factors produce. And anxious, stressed children can experience problems in school. So look at home first to see if there might be a correlation between what's happening there and what is happening at school.

Try to look back to see when the problems began. Do they coincide with the divorce or with the time your elderly aunt became very sick and then died? Or perhaps they began at the same time as conversations between you and your husband about money worries. This is what happened to a family we know:

> Loretta and her husband John spent long evenings talking quietly in the kitchen about what they might have to do if his business didn't pick up. They explored the possibility of selling the house and moving in with her parents in Florida. They also discussed moving to an apartment across town. They were very worried but felt strongly that their daughter shouldn't be part of their conversations. They didn't want her to worry, too.
>
> What they didn't know was that Megan overheard parts of the conversations and worried a great deal, so much so that her schoolwork began to suffer.

WHAT YOU CAN DO

Children need to be brought into conversations about matters that will have an impact on their lives. Loretta and John didn't need to tell Megan what their bank balance was, but they should have explained in a way she could understand that the family was having some financial problems. They could have assured her that they were doing everything they could to stay in their home, and they could also have asked Megan to help them save money. By communicating with her they would have had an opportunity to hear and answer her concerns.

It's also a good idea to share information with the teacher. While you don't have to tell her your bank balance or any personal details, we have found it helpful to let her know there's a problem. In fact, we've been scolded at times by some of our favorite teachers for not sharing information early enough! When the teacher knows what is going on, she can be on the alert for problems even before they start.

IS YOUR CHILD OVERSCHEDULED?

Some children who are not working up to their capabilities are, quite simply, burned out. Sometimes they are called "hurried" children—children who do too much, are pushed too hard (or push themselves too hard), or feel overwhelmed. These can include children whose every waking moment is programmed for one activity or another. Take Richard, for example:

Richard was a typical second grader. He was an average student who liked school and had many friends. He was polite to the teacher and always participated in class.

Both of Richard's parents worked, and he and his sister were cared for by a live-in nanny who took them to all their after-school activities. In November, his parents signed Richard up for a swimming team that practiced five days a week, sometimes before and other times after school, in addition to the piano lessons he took one afternoon, the karate lessons another day, and Cub Scouts one evening a week.

Richard's sister had a similar schedule, and often their nanny took them for a bite to eat in between events. Several nights a week they did not get home until 8:30 or so.

For Richard, the swimming practice was the straw that broke the camel's back. It was just too much for him. He appeared lethargic in class, his homework was not up to par, he was irritable to his friends, and his grades were suffering.

WHAT YOU CAN DO

Richard and his sister both needed to cut back on their after-school activities. While each activity may have grown out of their genuine interests, the total was too much, at least for Richard. Sometimes this happens without our even noticing, especially with bright, energetic children who have a lot of interests.

A good approach is to let your child choose for himself which activities to drop and which to continue. If he's severely overwhelmed, it might even be necessary to drop everything extra for a while. A first grader we know said that she was just too tired to do anything after school. Her mom wisely listened and cancelled all the activities for which they had signed up.

Another good idea is to schedule downtime—time to relax, read, watch TV, rest, snack, or whatever. An hour every afternoon without any pressures at all can be a wonderful restorative, especially for children who feel overburdened.

IS YOUR CHILD A LATE BLOOMER?

Most school districts in the United States, despite a wealth of research and practical experience to the contrary, group children according to chronological age. They do this for one reason: It is easier to group all five-year-olds in kindergarten, all six-year-olds in first grade, and so on.

Many child development experts feel, however, that children should be grouped according to their *developmental* age. They believe that teachers could be more effective working with children who are at the same, or approximately the same, point in their development. With chronological placement, a classroom of twenty-five children may actually contain five or six groups with differing developmental needs.

Perhaps your child is inches shorter than his peers, slighter in frame, and less agile. Or maybe he's socially immature and has a hard time separating from you. Even after several weeks of school, you may notice that he's still miserable when you part in the morning.

Frequently, a child does poorly in school because he is too young developmentally for the work required. If your school system assigns children to a grade chronologically, your child may be having trouble just because he isn't ready.

What You Can Do

If you are in doubt about your child's readiness for school, you might say you'll hold her back—lots of people do that. In some areas, holding back has become almost fashionable; some parents believe the extra year before school will put their children at the head of the class, straight on the track to an Ivy League school. But in most areas the practice of holding children back is not that widespread—although talking about it is. One mother's story illustrates how difficult the decision can be:

> Ben was born in September, one month premature. He was a small baby—only four and a half pounds. Gaining weight was hard for him, and at ten he's still considerably smaller than his friends. I'd noticed in both the gymnastics and swim classes we had taken together when he was a toddler how difficult it was for him to do some of the things that his peers did with ease.
>
> I met with Ben's nursery school teachers the spring before he was to enter kindergarten. The teachers told me he had trouble with both his fine motor skills—just holding a crayon was hard for him—and with his gross motor skills.
>
> I was not surprised with either assessment, but I was taken aback when they told me he had less control than most of the other students. Ben, they said, could not stay seated during reading time, and when he did sit down, he called out responses to other children's questions. They suggested I consider holding him back. I was crushed. All of Ben's friends were going into kindergarten in September; how would he feel not being with them? And to be honest, I wondered how I would feel.

Our friend's feelings were not unusual. She decided to meet with the principal of the school Ben would be attending. She asked questions about the kindergarten curriculum to see if it was *developmentally appropriate*. Her son's teachers explained what that meant and told her what to look for when she visited the kindergarten class. (A developmentally appropriate curriculum is designed to meet the individual needs of the wide range of developmental ages in the class. In other words, it provides learning and growth experiences for the child who is reading at five and for the child like Ben who needs practice to master the balance beam. The National Association for the Education of Young Children publishes a guide for parents and others to use when evaluating the appropriateness of a curriculum. We've listed it at the end of the chapter.)

After visiting the classroom and talking to the principal, I was no closer to knowing what to do. The classroom, to my untrained eyes, seemed good. What the principal said to me made sense, too. She suggested that there was no reason for me to make the decision immediately. She said that Ben would probably have great growth spurts over the summer. She also said I could wait until late August to make the decision. After all, it was a public school system, and Ben's space had to be there in September.

Following the principal's advice, our friend put off deciding what to do but kept her options open by enrolling Ben in a private kindergarten program for September.

Over the spring and the summer I did see Ben develop, but by August I could see that he was still far behind his friends. I went back to talk to the principal, who referred me to two parents—one who had held back her daughter and another who had not. And I talked to Ben's nursery school teacher again.

Our friend wasn't atypical. Dozens of parents each year struggle with this decision. They weigh the issues, read as much as they can, and talk to many people. Ultimately, though, the decision is theirs to make.

My decision to hold Ben back wasn't an easy one. While all the advice I received was good, when I weighed the pros and cons, I finally went with my gut feeling that Ben was just not ready.

This mother chose a private transitional kindergarten for him because of its accreditation by the state's department of education. Her state had a regulation that if a child attended any accredited kindergarten program, even a private one, the child was then eligible for first grade the following year. (By the way, Ben didn't go into first grade the next year.)

Another parent who worried about making this decision said, "This is a decision you second-guess for the rest of your child's school life. If you hold him back and he has problems in school, you blame yourself for delaying his entry. And if you don't hold him back and he fails a spelling test in third grade, you blame yourself, too. There's really no right or wrong answer."

Readiness for school is not the only time developmental issues arise with children. They can come up at any time. Sometimes they aren't apparent until later; sometimes we just don't see them. The first thing you need to do if you think your child might be a late bloomer is figure out the area in which her development lags. Are her problems physical, social, emotional, or academic? Refer to the questions we posed at the beginning of this chapter to help you sort this out.

With your notes in hand, talk with the teacher or a member of the school support staff to get ideas about how you can help strengthen the area or areas that need it. Talk to other parents who are going through similar difficulties or who have already worked through them with an older child. Physical difficulties might be lessened through involvement in a sports activity, for example. Social problems might be helped by scheduling play dates with a classmate suggested by the teacher—one with whom your child appears to relate well in class.

One way parents can support their child's emotional immaturity is by respecting it. It certainly doesn't help your child to hear, "Linda, don't be a crybaby! None of your friends is crying now. Be a big girl like everyone else." Linda isn't like everyone else, nor do you want her to be. You can encourage her independence by allowing her to be dependent when she needs to; that will give her the security to be more independent when she's ready.

If your child is having academic difficulties, we've given dozens of suggestions on fun learning activities in Chapter 4. Refer to them and to our advice to make reading a priority in your child's life. Nowhere do we suggest that you push your child; just give him more support and practice in the area(s) in which his development is delayed.

More and more school districts have begun to establish multiage classes to meet the varied developmental needs of students. For example, one multiage class might contain first and second graders and another second and third graders.

While they have many advantages, a central one is that such classes can help to address developmental differences among participating children. They take into consideration the fact that all seven-year-olds are not at the same level just because they're seven years old; nor is each seven-year-old at the same level in every area. An academically precocious eight-year-old might have the physical and emotional maturity of a six-year-old.

You might want to talk to your child's teacher or principal about the possibility of initiating a multiage class if you think your child would benefit from such an approach.

If neither shows any interest in exploring the possibility, try talking to the district person in charge of curriculum and instruction. Perhaps multiage classes could be the topic of a PTA meeting if enough parents are interested.

IS YOUR CHILD BORED?

We've known a number of children who weren't working up to their potential because they weren't challenged enough in school. It seems that some children just can't be bothered completing work that they find too easy. Or they breeze through their schoolwork, leaving it sloppy and in-accurate, and reserve their intelligence and energy for something else of their choosing—playing computer games, collecting stamps, or writing in a diary.

Ten-year-old David was an informed and avid collector of comic books. He used every bit of his allowance and whatever money he received for his birthday to add to his collection. He read adult magazines for collectors, seemed to store up information by the trunkload, and could talk in a mature, knowledgeable way about his collection—what he had and what he was looking for.

Yet in school David wasn't doing well at all. He was listless, rarely contributed to class or group discussions, and turned in slapdash, superficial work. When questioned, he complained that school was boring.

WHAT YOU CAN DO

If this is your child, you probably recognized him right away: an extremely bright, motivated, self-driven child outside school who is not functioning well in school. This child frustrates his parents, who know how bright he is. And sometimes he fools his teachers, who don't know him as well.

To begin to reconnect David to school, his parents probably need to follow three strategies simultaneously.

First, they need to work with David's teacher to make school more challenging for him. The teacher might give him some individualized assignments that are a bit more difficult or that capture his interest. She might also try to capitalize on David's passion for comic books by asking him to do some kind of project or report to the class on comic books.

David's parents might have to push the teacher a little to get her to provide extra material for him; not all teachers are comfortable with this style of working. They might have to suggest ideas or even convince the teacher of David's level of intelligence, and they might have to follow up with a conference with the principal. But this is important. Sometimes schoolpeople and parents worry less about the obviously bright child than the one with learning deficits, saying "He'll make it on his own" about the former while mobilizing special services for the latter. In our opinion, this should never be seen as an either-or proposition. David needs help. He is in trouble in school, and the adults responsible for him must try whatever strategies they can.

Second, David's parents should continue to encourage and support his outside interests. They might also want to plan additional family activities that relate specifically to what David is learning in school in order to enrich his studies and increase his motivation.

Finally, David needs to learn to handle the boring parts of life. We've seen many children who expect to be entertained in school complaining that school is boring. Such children are prime candidates for being held accountable for household chores, being asked to redo sloppy homework, and losing privileges when they don't meet their responsibilities. We adults know that every job has boring parts as well, and we're doing our children a disservice if we don't hold them responsible for those parts of their work.

IS YOUR CHILD GIFTED?

It might seem that it would be easy to have a gifted child, that the kinds of problems we've been describing just wouldn't happen. But that's not the case at all. Parenting a gifted child frequently requires spending a great deal of time supporting and advocating in school for that child. Take the case of David. To his parents and friends, David was a bright and interesting youngster. It's even possible that he was gifted. What advice would we have for his parents if they thought that?

We would caution them not to rush to this conclusion. The truly gifted population is a very small percentage of the total population—anywhere from 2 to 5 percent, depending on whom you consult.

What does it mean to be gifted? There's an important distinction to make between *talented*, which refers to special abilities in particular areas such as music, sports, or visual arts, and *gifted*, which refers to superior intellectual abilities. Both gifted and talented youngsters can be among those who, like David, do poorly in school because they're bored.

In general, gifted and talented children can be recognized because they do things much earlier or noticeably better than their peers. The one-year-old who speaks in complete sentences and the six-year-old violin virtuoso are good examples. The books we've listed at the end of the chapter give more extensive guidelines, checklists, and resources parents can turn to for information and support.

What You Can Do

We would advise David's parents to get help—from experts and from other parents. The school district should be able to direct them to an expert, either a district employee or an outside consultant, who can help determine whether David is really gifted and recommend appropriate educational options. Other parents in the district might have a support group or network to help each other, because gifted and talented children *are* different. They need more challenges than the typical classroom can provide, they're not always accepted by other children, and they can be difficult to raise.

If it was determined that David was indeed gifted or talented, his parents would want to do everything possible to help him reach his potential, both in and outside of school. This is exactly what all of us want to do for our children. David's parents might look for outside activities that tap into his talents, like art lessons at the Y, a specialized summer camp, or a community center children's theater group. They might plan family outings to encourage his interests.

In addition, they would have to thoroughly investigate the district's offerings for gifted and talented children. If you're looking into this for your child, you might want to ask questions like these:

• Are gifted children pulled out of regular classrooms for the program? How often and for how long? Or are they separated into their own classroom for the entire day?

• What kind of activities go on in the program? Are they fast-paced and challenging? Do they enrich the regular curriculum or teach entirely new subjects? Do they stress problem-solving skills and creativity?

• How many children are in the program? Are they representative of the school population in terms of race, ethnicity, and gender?

• How are the children selected? Are test scores used? (If you find that test scores are used to exclude children—that is, a child scoring below a certain point cannot join the program—you might want to object, since, as we've discussed, test scores are poor indicators of ability.) Do teachers have the chance to recommend children? Are parents consulted? Are talents other than intellectual ability considered?

• Who is the teacher? What kind of special training does he or she have?

IS YOUR CHILD A NONCONFORMING LEARNER?

Sometimes children have problems in school because of mismatches between their learning styles and the way new information is presented to them. The notion that sometimes instruction should be adapted to the child is a fairly new one. When we were in elementary school, it was up to the *child* to adapt to *school*, not the other way around; and this is still the case in many schools and classrooms.

What is *learning style* all about? Simply this: Each of us has a set of conditions under which we learn most effectively, as well as our own individual combination of strengths and weaknesses. While one of us might be able to work only in a very quiet room, for example, another might concentrate best with the radio playing or even in the midst of family activities. Some of us are at our peak in the morning, others in the afternoon or evening.

Learning style preferences encompass a broad range of conditions, including these:

- *Lighting*—bright or dim
- *Temperature*—cool or warm
- *Seating*—in a hard, upright chair or a soft, sprawling chair or sofa; sitting still versus moving around
- *Time of day*—morning versus afternoon
- *Learning modality*—hearing, seeing, or hands-on manipulation as a preferred way of receiving new information
- *Grouping and interaction*—working alone, with a partner, or in a small group; competition versus cooperation; independent versus dependent work
- *Thinking style*—logical, detailed, step-by-step thinking, often called left brain thinking, versus intuitive, creative, holistic thinking, or right brain thinking

Suppose your son is not a morning person. He's slow to start in the morning, finds it hard to concentrate, and tends to stare out the window, daydreaming, almost until lunchtime. But by then the main instructional periods for reading and math are over for the day.

Or perhaps your daughter is an extremely active child who finds it almost painful to sit still at her desk for long periods of time. At home she reads and watches TV lying on the floor or hanging upside down from a chair. In school she fidgets, taps her foot almost incessantly, and calls out answers instead of waiting to be called on.

You might notice another child who is most successful working in a small cooperative group. Here she's an obvious leader, is very creative, and has quite high standards.

Working alone, on the other hand, she rushes through assignments and is satisfied with rather sloppy work.

Are these careless children or children who aren't trying? There was a time when the answer almost universally would have been yes. Now, although individual teachers might still choose to look no further, most experts would agree that it's worthwhile to explore learning style issues in cases like these.

WHAT YOU CAN DO

You probably know more about your child's learning style than the teacher does. For one thing, you see your child in more varied situations, and for another, you are more focused on your child than the teacher can be. So even though you may never have thought about learning styles per se, you are probably well aware of when, where, and how your child concentrates best.

Take homework time, for example. We have found this to be a good time to observe our children's styles of working. Think about how you've arrived at decisions about when, where, and how homework gets done. Or if homework seems to entail a nightly battle in your home, you may find that learning style issues are the culprit. See if you can answer the following questions or if they perhaps raise some new considerations. If you've noticed that your son gets antsy while doing homework, for example, you might want to try letting him take a break halfway through. Do his concentration and work improve? If so, build in time for a break from now on.

• What have you found to be the most effective time for your child to do homework: right after school; later, after a TV or play break; or even later, after dinner? Some children can't relax or go on to other activities until their homework is done. Others can't concentrate on homework without first taking a break.

• Does your child work best in a quiet spot with no distractions, or does he like to be right in the middle of things, perhaps with the radio playing?

• Does he finish all his homework in one sitting, or does he need a break?

• Does he have any trouble copying down the assignments? This may indicate that he's an auditory learner, meaning that he learns best what he *hears*. It may also be a signal that his visual skills need to be strengthened. Some board games such as Memory, Concentration, and Monopoly can help with this.

• Does your child get right to work on his own, or does he ask for help before trying? The latter may mean he's a dependent learner who requires a lot of reassurance. Teachers and parents need to help dependent learners increase their self-confidence and ability to work alone, while still providing the needed support.

• Does he have trouble consistently with one subject area or type of assignment? He may need extra help or even tutoring in this one area. The teacher can suggest appropriate help or give individualized assignments with which you can help him.

• How does he handle long-term assignments? Does he leave them until the last minute? Does he need help budgeting time or planning? Most children do! Remember, even most adults tend to procrastinate, so don't be too hard on your ten-year-old when he does, too!

Jot down your observations, being as specific as you can. Now make an appointment with the teacher and share your observations with her.

WHAT THE TEACHER CAN DO

In every instance we have cited, a few minor adjustments in instruction can make dramatic differences for your child. For your son who is at his best after lunch, there's no law that says reading and math must always be taught in the morning. How about morning one day and afternoon the next? That would accommodate all the children's best times of day. For your daughter the fidgeter, being allowed to get up and move around or to sit on the floor or in a beanbag chair could greatly increase her concentration and attention span. And for the child who excels in cooperative groups, we believe that every class should include meaningful cooperative learning projects.

Good teachers usually teach using different modalities, sometimes even without thinking about it. That's why they explain new information several different ways. The child who learns through hands-on experiences—using the sense of touch, physically manipulating objects—is most likely to be shortchanged in the typical classroom. But even the child who's an auditory learner can experience some difficulties, since most instruction still depends heavily on visual skills. In these cases, your intervention may be needed to urge the teacher to accommodate differing learning styles.

FURTHER READING

James Alvino. *Parents' Guide to Raising a Gifted Child: Recognizing and Developing Your Child's Potential.* Boston: Little, Brown, 1985.

Sue Bredekamp, editor. *Developmentally Appropriate Practice in Early Childhood Programs Serving Children from Birth Through Age 8.* Washington, DC:

National Association for the Education of Young Children, 1987.

Rita Dunn and Shirley A. Griggs. *Learning Styles: Quiet Revolution in American Secondary Schools.* Reston, VA: National Association of Secondary School Principals, 1988.

Virginia Ehrlich. *Gifted Children: A Guide for Parents and Teachers.* Englewood Cliffs, NJ: Prentice-Hall, 1982.

David Elkind. *The Hurried Child: Growing Up Too Fast Too Soon,* rev. ed. New York: Addison-Wesley, 1988.

Howard Gardner. *Frames of Mind: The Theory of Multiple Intelligences.* New York: Basic Books, 1983.

Arnold Gesell, Frances L. Ilg, and Louise Bates Ames. *The Child from Five to Ten.* New York: Harper and Row, 1977.

Lawrence T. Greene. *Kids Who Underachieve.* New York: Simon and Schuster, 1986.

James W. Keefe. *Learning Style: Theory and Practice.* Reston, VA: National Association of Secondary School Principals, 1987.

Barbara Kuczen. *Childhood Stress.* New York: Delacorte Press, 1982.

Karen Miller. *Ages and Stages.* Marshfield, MA: Telshare, 1985.

Rosemary Peterson and Victoria Felton-Collins. *The Piaget Handbook for Teachers and Parents.* New York: Teachers College Press, 1986.

8

WHEN PROBLEMS DON'T GO AWAY

Sometimes, no matter what we do, our children's problems just don't go away. Whether it's difficulty with math, a lack of friends, general unhappiness with school, or dramatically disorganized homework, a persistent and unexplained problem requires us to investigate further.

We've already said that the first thing to do when you think there might be a serious problem is to be an extra-attentive audience—spend some time carefully observing your child and making notes about what you see. These specifics will be extremely helpful later when you're deciding what to do. In the preceding chapter, we suggested that developmental lags, divergent learning styles, the need for more challenges, or difficulties at home might be causing problems.

If you've talked to fellow parents, the teacher, or other school professionals and tried some strategies they have suggested, and you still believe there are problems, you might be right: Something else might be wrong. You might have to become an advocate and go to bat for your child.

As you try to pinpoint the problem, the following questions might be useful:

- What exactly do I see happening that makes me think there is a problem?
- When does this usually happen? Is there a pattern? Is it at a certain time of day? When my child is hungry or tired? When he has to do homework? When he encounters a math problem he can't solve? After he eats something sweet?
- How does my child react? Perhaps he bursts into tears, throws his papers across the floor, closes his books without doing the work, or moans, "I'm stupid. I just can't do this work!"
- How do I react? Does my reaction make things better or worse? Are there different reactions I could try?
- Is there something I might do to prevent the problem? Is there something I think the teacher might do?
- Does my child think there is a problem? Can he talk about it? What does he think is the cause? Does he have any ideas about solving it?

In this chapter, we look at some of the more serious problems we might find. We also explore what we parents can do about them. It's important to keep in mind that while all problems aren't fixable, it is usually possible to improve our children's situation. Remember, we know our children better than anyone else, and if we feel there is a problem, it is our right and our responsibility to investigate it.

LEARNING DISABILITIES

It might be that your son who had trouble copying down homework assignments or math problems continues to have that trouble. Maybe your daughter with the messy desk is losing her work and losing track of what she's doing. Or perhaps, despite extensive after-school tutoring, she's just not making any progress in reading and is falling further and further behind her classmates.

In these cases and in other instances where there's a persistent weakness, your child might have a learning disability. This term is bandied about and is used to label children as though everyone knows exactly what it means. The truth is that it's a catchall phrase used to describe a variety of learning difficulties, some mild and some serious. These include difficulties understanding or using written or spoken language but do not include problems due to mental retardation, emotional disturbance, or handicaps such as blindness or deafness.

One child might have difficulty with reading or writing when his verbal ability is normal. Another child might have trouble with organization and study skills. Others might have problems with spelling, math, or following multistep directions. Other children have difficulty with word retrieval—thinking of the right word to name specific objects or actions, despite knowing the word when they hear it.

You're probably familiar with a common learning disability: *attention deficit disorder* (ADD), formerly called hyperactivity. It is thought to affect more than ten percent of all elementary schoolchildren. It usually shows up between the ages of five and twelve, and for some reason is far more common among boys than girls. The child with ADD might be one who can't sit still, who is constantly fidgeting, who talks too much and doesn't listen, who calls out answers without being called on, or whose attention moves quickly from one topic to the next. In the classroom and on the playground, the child with ADD is disruptive and often in trouble.

Because it can be treated with medication (usually Ritalin) and changes in diet (less sugar and caffeine), ADD may well have a physical cause. Like the term learning disability, however, hyperactivity is sometimes used inappropriately as a catchall label. Be sure to get more than one opinion if this diagnosis is given to your child.

Learning disabilities are not always readily apparent in children. Often they're not diagnosed until the third or fourth grade and sometimes even later. One child we knew compensated so well for his organizational and retrieval difficulties that he wasn't identified as learning disabled until high school. His mother had always felt that there was a problem, though. When she gave him several tasks to complete, he couldn't remember them all, unlike his older brother. Teachers had dismissed her concerns by telling her that her son was very smart but was just lazy and sloppy. This reaction is not uncommon, especially when children are bright. We may think a child isn't trying hard enough or isn't paying attention, seeing him as a student who *will not* do his best when, in fact, he *cannot*.

Nearly all children have difficulty with some learning areas, so don't assume your child is learning disabled if he has some of these symptoms. Persistent or severe problems should trigger a closer look, however.

What You Can Do

We have seen more than one instance where the parents recognized that there was a problem long before the school did. If you suspect that your child has a learning disability, you need to be ready to spring into action.

First, talk about your concerns with the teacher, school psychologist, learning specialist, or someone else who knows your child well. This is where your careful observations and notes will really pay off because you'll have specific examples to talk about with them.

Second, make sure the teacher gets involved so that she doesn't continue to view your child inappropriately as lazy or sloppy.

Third, get your child professionally tested and diagnosed. This testing usually includes three things:

1. A comprehensive interview, covering family and health history
2. A battery of tests examining cognitive ability and achievement as well as other things such as coordination, attention span, and sensory processing
3. A psychological profile

The good news is that under the provisions of Public Law 94-142 (Individuals with Disabilities Education Act), the school district *must* provide this testing at no cost.

A family we know was very worried about their nine-year-old daughter who seemed to have a variety of language-related problems. She reversed letters and words (said "hot" for "cold"), had trouble putting tasks in the proper sequence, and had fallen behind her classmates in her reading and writing achievement. The school kept reassuring her parents that Rebecca's problems weren't serious, but they didn't agree.

In desperation they were about to have a private consultant do extensive tests at a cost of $600 or $700, which they could ill afford. They didn't know that the school district was obligated to do this testing until a friend told them. When they asked, the district finally tested Rebecca. The results? They were right: Rebecca was clearly language impaired and needed extra help from the school's speech and reading teachers.

If your child is diagnosed with a learning disability, you need to talk with the specialists in school who are working with her to find out what you can do at home. You will probably find that you need to provide a great deal of support to help her succeed in school. You may need to supervise homework closely, help her review work aloud, structure her long-term assignments such as research papers or book reports into step-by-step tasks, or spend extra time with her going over reading or math work. Children with learning disabilities can learn to compensate for them quite well—but not without help.

WHAT THE TEACHER CAN DO

Most of the time, learning disabled children stay in their regular classrooms. Sometimes they are taken out for extra help; sometimes a special teacher works with them right in the classroom. Only those with very severe disabilities need to be in a special class all the time, and there's a lot of debate about that. The regular classroom teacher's role is critical, therefore.

As we said earlier, it's important to get the teacher involved from the start so that he understands what is really going on with your child. Because learning disabled children generally have average or above-average intelligence, they can be quite confusing to the regular teacher, who often has little or no special training in this area. In our experience, it's important to make sure that the teacher gets help in setting appropriate expectations for your child. The learning specialist, reading teacher, or resource room teacher who works with your child can help you with this process—usually an ongoing one. Don't be surprised if the teacher doesn't understand the situation right away. But don't let up; his attitude toward and treatment of your child, if it's inappropriate, can be very damaging.

SPECIAL EDUCATION

There are times when our children's lack of progress in school is more serious even than learning disabilities. If our children are mentally retarded, emotionally disturbed, have severe learning disorders, or are physically handicapped, they have special learning needs. By law, all school districts are obligated to fulfill these.

In 1975, as a result of extensive and persistent lobbying on the part of parents and special education activists, Congress passed Public Law 94-142, the Education of All Handicapped Children Act (now known as the Individuals with Disabilities Education Act). This law mandates that public schools provide a free, appropriate public education in the least restrictive environment possible for children who need special services. It also mandates that related services be provided, such as early identification and assessment of the handicap, speech and hearing therapy, physical and occupational therapy, counseling, diagnostic medical services, and transportation.

What does this mean to parents? In simple language, it means that by law our children are guaranteed an education regardless of their handicapping condition. Parents can refer their child to their district's Committee on Special Education if they have reason to believe that their child needs special services. A school employee who believes a child needs special education services can also refer the child to the committee.

Maria, a second grader, wore braces on her legs because she suffered from cerebral palsy. She was bright as could be but was not able to go up and down stairs. When her mother met with the Committee on Special Education, she asked that Maria be placed in a regular class and be given assistance negotiating the stairs in the morning, at lunchtime, after school, and in case of a fire. The committee agreed and asked for her to be assigned to a special bus with a moving lift. The school district was able to accommodate these requests and placed Maria in the least restrictive environment—a regular classroom.

Around the country, more and more special education children are being placed in regular classrooms when that's appropriate to their needs. This is due mostly to pressure from their parents. Educators are finding that this movement toward *inclusion* benefits all children, because they learn to accept and deal with one another's differences. It works best, of course, when teachers are well prepared to work with diverse learning styles and needs.

The rights of children and parents are protected under the law. In fact, the school district should give parents a list of their rights. By law, there is also a timetable the district *must* follow that dictates the events that must occur once a referral is made.

WHERE YOU CAN FIND OUT MORE

The first place to contact for information and guidance is your school district, which probably has a whole department devoted to special education. When you talk to the staff there, ask for the names and telephone numbers of parents with children in special education who have agreed to talk with other parents. Here are some questions you might want to ask them:

- How long has your child been in the special education program? What kind of progress has he made? Is this progress what you expected? Is it reasonable, given his disability?
- What special services is your child getting? How satisfied are you with these services?
- Is the school responsive when you have a question or problem? Do school personnel involve you regularly in assessing your child's progress?
- How does your child feel about being in special education? Does he have friends who are not in special education? How is his social life in general?
- With what are you most dissatisfied? With what are you most happy?

Find out if your district has a special education advisory committee or a support group for parents with children in the program and consider joining one of them. In these groups, you'll be able to talk to parents who have been involved in the program for a while. It's probably worth attending a couple of meetings before you decide whether or not to join. Find out how often they meet and for how long, what kinds of topics they discuss, whether school personnel or outside experts participate, and how structured the meetings are. If the meetings sound like random conversations with no focus, you may decide you don't want to give up evenings with your family for them. On the other hand, perhaps you will welcome the opportunity simply to converse with other parents.

SCHOOL FAILURE

Every year in the United States, usually in the spring, millions of parents are told that their children are being recommended for retention. This is particularly shocking since most current research studies conclude that retention is not all it's cracked up to be. It is not a gift of time, as some suggest, but rather can produce social and emotional problems, including poor self-esteem. Children who are retained may feel a profound sense of failure even if they're very young.

Research also shows that the chances of dropping out of school in later years are dramatically increased for children who are held back. The academic achievement of retained students is lower than that of peers who were performing similarly but were not held back.

WHAT YOU CAN DO

There are some things you can and should do if you receive the upsetting news that the school wants to retain your child. You may have to act quickly before the school year ends.

The first thing to do is talk with your child. You don't want to upset her, but you do want to alert her to the fact that her teacher thinks there are some problems. The one thing you don't want to do is make her think she's stupid.

Tell her you're going to meet with the teacher and ask her what she thinks the problem is.

Second, set up a meeting with the principal and the teacher. This is an opportunity to learn what the school's intentions are. You might begin like this:

> This news was a surprise to me, and I'm very upset. Why do you want to retain my child? I don't understand why this is the first time I've heard anything about my child having serious problems.

Then you might want to find out more about the difficulties your child is having. Press the teacher for specific details by asking questions such as the following:

- What subject areas is my child doing poorly in—all of them or just certain ones?
- What evidence do you have for this?
- What has the school already done to try to help her?
- Are you seeing problems with her behavior, too? What kind of problems? Can you give me some specific examples?
- Have you given my child any tests—for learning disabilities or psychological problems? Do you plan to? (A school is required to get a parent's written permission before it can do this testing.)

> I was devastated by the news that the school wanted to hold Janine back, but I was going to accept their decision because I thought they knew what was best for her. My friend insisted that I look into it further. "They're not always right," she said.
>
> So I went to the local college's education library and with the help of the librarian found many articles on retention. I was surprised at the number! I learned that there are

several alternatives to retention, such as summer tutoring, a partial retention in which the child moves on with the rest of her class but returns to the lower grade for specific skill instruction, and other special strategies (such as one-on-one lessons with the reading teacher), enabling the child to move on to the next grade.

When I met with the teacher and principal, I asked if they had considered these. They were surprised that I was so well informed, but they were open to my ideas. Together we decided on a rigorous summer tutorial and agreed to reevaluate Janine in the fall to see if she needed more help. But she would move on with her class.

I can't tell you how grateful I am to my friend!

All stories don't end quite so happily, of course. Sometimes the principal and teacher are determined to retain your child. In that case, you'll want to ask what plans they have to support her. All too often the school thinks that merely repeating the grade will solve the problem. Ask questions such as these:

- If my child is retained, will she be placed in a special program or in a regular class?
- Will she have the same teacher she had this year or another one?
- Will there be an educational plan for her? Will this be a written one?
- What kind of extra help will she receive? How will you address her specific difficulties?

If you agree with the school's decision—whether it's retention or promotion—ask them for a *detailed, written plan* outlining the specific steps they plan to take to ensure your child's success. Tell them that you would like to be part of designing that plan, and schedule another meeting for that purpose.

If the school insists upon retention and you still believe it's not in your child's best interests, ask the principal how and to whom you can appeal this decision. Usually you can go to the district superintendent or an assistant superintendent in charge of pupil services or instruction.

One parent accepted the school's decision to hold her son back but thought that if she moved him to a new school, it would be easier for him. What she didn't realize was that his records would follow him to the new school and, at nine years old, his self-esteem would suffer. Another parent told us how she tried to help her son salvage his self-esteem:

When I learned my child was going to be retained, I knew I had to talk to him about it, but I didn't know what words to use. So first I talked to our pediatrician for advice on what to say. She was very helpful and prepared me for staying calm and letting him cry. She said that until he got the hurt out of his system, we couldn't move on. It was hard, but I followed her advice.

I sat him down after dinner one night and talked to him about the meeting I had had with the teacher and the principal. "They think you would do better if you repeat second grade," I told him. "After thinking about it, I agree." As you can imagine, Billy cried, promised to do better, and begged me to let him stay with his friends. I listened and hugged him and assured him that he could play with his buddies at lunchtime and after school. I promised to help him with his schoolwork, too. "You are not stupid," I said. "You just need a little more time in second grade. That's what you can tell your friends."

We didn't finish our discussion in one sitting, of course. But I repeated the same messages each time we talked about it, and I think Billy came to terms with it.

Regardless of what decision is made, it's important to stay on top of the situation. Schedule meetings with the principal and the teacher throughout the following year.

KEEPING A POSITIVE ATTITUDE

We're not going to minimize the pain involved when your child is diagnosed with a learning disability or other special education need or is retained in school.

> After the teacher told me that Joe had a learning disability, I had to go to work. I sat on the train, crying quietly all the way into the city. My feelings ran the gamut from pain to disappointment to fear. I don't know what the other passengers thought was happening to me; I didn't even see them. I just kept imagining how hard life was going to be for Joe. I felt that somehow I had failed him.

In our society, it is no small thing to be labeled, to be different. Unless your school is very unusual, your son's friends will know that he's getting extra help and might even make fun of him for that. The second-grade daughter of a friend came running to her mother when her playmate told her, "I'm smarter than you are because I don't go to Mrs. Rosenberg [the learning specialist] like you do." Our friend was lucky: This happened in her home, and she was right there to talk to both girls. Such incidents happen more often on the school playground, at lunch, or on the soccer field when we're not around. This makes it all the more important for us to provide support and encouragement for our children. If we don't have a positive attitude, chances are our children won't, either.

Now that educators know so much more about learning

problems—and children are benefiting from this knowledge—many more role models exist that show what children can achieve even with severe disabilities. Chris Burke, who has Down's syndrome, has surprised many a skeptic with his ability to keep up with ABC's weekly television show *Life Goes On.* Many famous and accomplished Americans have been able to overcome learning disabilities on the road to greatness. And people who live normal lives with a range of disabilities regularly appear on the children's television show *Sesame Street.*

All these accomplishments are possible with a positive attitude and a good education. Much of that depends on you and how you advocate for your child.

FURTHER READING

Lisa J. Bain. *A Parent's Guide to Attention Deficit Disorders.* New York: Delta Books, 1991.

Nancy Berla. "Retention in Grade: Failing Students or Failing to Meet Students' Needs?" *NCCE Network for Public Schools,* 17:1 (1991).

Jill Bloom. *Help Me to Help My Child: A Sourcebook for Parents of Learning Disabled Children.* Boston: Little, Brown, 1990.

Deidre Hayden. *Negotiating the Special Education Maze.* Englewood Cliffs, NJ: Prentice-Hall, 1982.

Harold N. Levinson and Addie Sanders. *The Upside-Down Kids: Helping Dyslexic Children Understand Themselves and Their Disorder.* New York: M. Evans, 1991.

National Association of School Psychologists. *Student Grade Retention.* Position Statement, 1988.

Betty Osman. *Learning Disabilities: A Family Affair.* New York: Random House, 1979.

Kenneth Shore. *The Special Education Handbook: A Com-*

prehensive Guide for Parents and Educators. New York: Teachers College Press, 1986.

Eileen Simpson. *Reversals: A Personal Account of Victory Over Dyslexia.* New York: Noonday Press, 1991.

RESOURCES

Council for Exceptional Children
1920 Association Drive
Reston, VA 22901
703-620-3660

Federation for Children with Special Needs
95 Berkeley Street, Suite 104
Boston, MA 02116
617-482-2915

Learning Disability Association of America
4156 Library Road
Pittsburgh, PA 15234
412-341-1515

National Association of School Psychologists
8455 Colesville Road, Suite 1000
Silver Spring, MD 20910
301-608-0500

National Center for Learning Disabilities
99 Park Avenue
New York, NY 10016
212-687-7211

National Information Center for Children
    and Youth with Disabilities
P. O. Box 1492
Washington, DC 20013
800-999-5599

Orton Dyslexia Society
The Chester Building, Suite 382
Baltimore, MD 21286
410-296-0232

9

NEW OPPORTUNITIES
FOR PARENTS

Most of this book focuses on ways that we can directly support and advocate for our own children in school. We emphasize these roles because we believe that they are the most important, especially in the early years of school. If you have limited time and have to make choices, as we've said many times, you'll probably want to focus first on your child's immediate needs.

But there are broader roles we parents can play, too—perhaps when our children are older, when they're secure and need less help with their schoolwork, when we have more time, or when we're comfortable with taking on new challenges. In fact, the concept of parent involvement has taken on new and expanded meanings in recent years, and our book would not be complete if we didn't take a look at some of these broader opportunities for parent participation.

Among the roles we explore here are how we can participate in school governance, what it means to be able to choose our children's schools, and how we can become activists for change. Finally, we define what it means to hold schools truly accountable. These opportunities might not be open to you yet in your local schools, but they're coming! We are convinced that these are the directions in which the majority of schools will be heading over the next decade.

This is a time of change in public education, and one reason is that nowadays we parents have the chance to make a difference—if we choose—in ways that were not open to parents just a few years ago.

SCHOOL-BASED MANAGEMENT AND SHARED DECISION MAKING

In the "old days," schools rarely solicited or even welcomed parents' ideas about educational matters. Fortunately, those barriers are beginning to break down as school personnel start to recognize that they need us and as we parents come to realize that we have key contributions to make to our children's success in school.

One of the most visible new roles parents are taking in schools is at the forefront of school governance reform. In growing numbers of school governing councils, which are composed of elected representatives of all the school constituencies—teachers, administrators and other staff, parents, and sometimes even students—parents participate in running the school, helping to make decisions about programs, personnel, and budget.

This is part of the movement toward *school-based management* (SBM) and *shared decision making* (SDM) that is sweeping the country. Although big and small districts, urban and suburban, are trying out SBM and SDM, there is still much confusion about what is entailed. In school-based management, decisions are made by the school instead of the district office. Shared decision making in its purest sense

means that representatives of all constituencies affected by
decisions have a voice in making them. Most of the time,
schools combine school-based management and shared decision making by establishing school governing councils.

These councils often start out with confusion and conflict,
as everyone learns new skills and new roles. This is sometimes most difficult for parents, who can feel like outsiders.
Here is one mother's initial experience:

> When our school started a governing council, I thought
> it was a natural extension of my work on the PTA, so I ran
> for one of the parent seats. That was the easy part. The
> hard part was sitting at council meetings, not really sure of
> my place. Was I there as a token? Did the schoolpeople
> really want to hear what I thought? Could I be really honest?
> What would happen to my son if I said what I thought?
>
> I also wondered why everything took so long. I sometimes
> wanted to say, "Why are you people making such a big deal
> about this? Just do it!" It often seemed to me that there
> was endless debate about unimportant details.

This parent wasn't alone in her confusion and frustra-
tion. School staff also had questions about the governing
council:

> I was "volunteered" to run for a teacher seat on the
> governing council its first year because nobody else would
> do it. Sometimes I think my colleagues were smarter than
> I was. We meet and meet and meet and don't accomplish
> anything. It seems as though we spend half of the time
> listening to the principal and the other half answering par-
> ents' questions. We don't even know what our responsibil-
> ities are.

These reactions are a normal part of the change process. This is why school councils frequently use outside facilitators (consultants or district staff) to help them work through the conflict, build teamwork, and train them in district policies and procedures.

That same mother said later in the year, "It was really exciting when we finally made our first big decision: to start an after-school program. Then we got to watch it become a reality step by step." The teacher who had complained in the beginning talked to us later in the year about how he came to view parents differently:

> One day when we were arguing about something—I don't even remember what—a parent on the council suddenly said, "Whoa! Stop!" Everyone looked at her, shocked. "We shouldn't be arguing," she told us. "We want the same thing. We parents just want our children to do well in school, and I think you do, too." The rest of us realized that, simplistic as it sounded, she was right. We looked around the table, and for the first time we didn't see each other as adversaries.
>
> After that we tried to begin our discussions with a reminder of our goals. It helped.

There are also some real success stories, as told by this principal:

> Ever since I became principal, I wanted to try multiage classes. But I knew there was a lot of resistance to the idea from parents and some staff, mostly based on misinformation and fear. Quite frankly, I wasn't willing to take the issue on alone.
>
> When the school governing council was established, that was my chance. I took my idea to them and explained why

I thought it would work. They agreed even though I warned them there would be a fight.

We planned and carried out a communications blitz guided by a parent member who worked in public relations. We sent home several written explanations of the idea, made presentations at faculty and PTA meetings, and held informal coffees at parents' homes. All of this culminated in an evening meeting of the entire school community to hash out the idea. While resisters were there, they were far outnumbered by supporters, and the following year we piloted a six-, seven-, and eight-year-old class.

I really believe that I could not have succeeded alone. Without the support of the parents and staff on the governing council, my idea never would have been accepted.

As these examples show, school-based management and shared decision making are not easy. Trust, cooperation, patience, and the ability to understand the other person's point of view are all required in superhuman proportions. In schools where it's working, however, people say they can't imagine making decisions any other way. And it certainly provides parents with a potentially powerful voice in their children's schools.

SCHOOL CHOICE

Choice has recently become a fashionable concept in education, and one on which people from all points on the political spectrum seem to agree. In fact, on the face of it, it seems un-American to question the concept of choice. But as you might suspect, school choice means very different things to different people. So let's begin with some definitions.

For some, school choice means free market choice where

vouchers can be cashed in at any school one wants—private, parochial, or public. One of the arguments used to support this idea is that competition will force all schools to improve—an argument without any research evidence to back it up. Those opposed to this kind of choice believe that it will weaken the public schools by reducing the number of middle-class students. Furthermore, since vouchers can't possibly cover the full cost of private school tuition, we believe this kind of choice will benefit only those who can make up the difference.

For us and many others, it makes sense to talk about choice among public schools, either within a particular school district or across districts. Usually this means that students and their parents choose the schools they will attend at a particular level—elementary, junior high, or high school. With *controlled choice*, these are limited by certain specified factors, usually the need to maintain a racial and ethnic balance among schools. This is the case in our district, where all entering kindergartners attend the schools their parents have chosen, as long as the racial and ethnic make-up of each school is virtually the same as that of the others.

For public school choice to work well for children, parents need to be counseled so they can make informed decisions. In our district, as in many with choice, parents are urged to visit all the schools and ask questions such as those we suggested in Chapter 2. This means that everyone starts out more or less on equal ground.

The advantage of choice is that we parents have an opportunity to achieve a fit between the schools and our own beliefs about education as well as what we think our children need. One parent new to our district told us:

> I think it's so exciting to be able to choose a school. I meet parents all over the city, and everywhere the conversation is

the same: What schools have you visited? What did you see?
What do you think? Have you made up your mind yet?

It's amazing how my perceptions are different from other
parents'. Where I see a highly structured setting that would
be good for my son, another mother sees a rigid environment
that would destroy her child's independent spirit. Before I
started looking at schools, I didn't think I would see such
differences.

Choice in and of itself is neither fair nor unfair; as with
so many other educational ideas, it depends on how it's
carried out. Done with a great deal of care, school choice
can offer parents the opportunity to place their children in
the schools they think are best for them.

ACTIVISM FOR CHANGE

At times we parents feel frustrated by a decision made or
an action taken by a principal, the superintendent, or the
school board. Sometimes we might think, "Oh, well, the
school board has made a poor decision. I don't agree with
it, but I guess I can live with it." Other times we might
react quite differently; we might think the action or inaction
is something we can't live with at all. When that happens,
and we decide that we can't just sit around and do nothing,
we step into the role of activist. We might dash off a letter
of protest to the school board, or we might do what this
mother and father did:

> We happened to be at a school board meeting when the
> superintendent recommended eliminating the after-school
> intramural sports program. We were furious. He said that
> the district was in bad financial shape and could save more

than $200,000 by cutting this program. When it came time for public comments, we voiced our strong objections. The superintendent and school board members listened politely and thanked us for our comments. We didn't care about their thanks; we were angry. To our twins, the sports program meant everything. We couldn't afford private swimming and ice hockey lessons on our salaries. Neither could most of the families on the teams.

Ben and Helen Smith didn't know exactly what to do, but they knew they had to do something to save their district's sports program. They remembered when during their college days they had organized a protest over the denial of tenure to one of their favorite professors. They had started with a small group of friends in a letter-writing and petition campaign and ended by making a presentation to the college's board of trustees in support of the professor. It had worked then—the professor got tenure. They thought it might work now to save the sports program. They knew there was power in numbers.

We decided that we couldn't waste any time, so we created some flyers that very night. The next day we distributed them to all the parents and students at an after-school practice. The flyers described the proposed cuts and announced a meeting at our house on Saturday morning. We had no idea that we would get the response we did: Roughly thirty-five parents showed up to find out what they could do! Like us, they were outraged by the proposed elimination of the sports program.

The parents, with Helen Smith acting as informal chair, talked about how important the program was to their children and considered strategies they might use to persuade the superintendent and school board to look elsewhere for

cuts. The first thing they decided to do was send a small
representative group to meet with the superintendent and
the athletic director. They wanted to hear the specifics of
the proposal and find out if there was any willingness to
discuss alternatives.

> The meeting was frustrating. It was apparent soon after
> we got there that the superintendent was just humoring us
> and that he and the athletic director had no intention of
> working with us. Their minds were already made up.
> So we put the second part of our campaign into operation
> and divided into teams to go to each of the dozen or so
> intramural games that took place daily. Most parents in our
> town don't go to the games because they work, so we had
> to depend on the kids to deliver our message. We sent a
> petition home with each of the students and asked them to
> get their parents' signatures and an additional twenty sig-
> natures by the next school board meeting, a week away.

The parents and students didn't let the Smiths and their
group down. By the following week more than two thousand
signatures had been collected. In addition, the board received more than fifty letters praising the sports program
and requesting its continuation. The president of the board
accepted the petitions and told the group that she or the
superintendent would contact them in the next few days.

> We were pleased but skeptical when the superintendent
> said he wanted to meet with four or five of the parents from
> our group to talk about the sports program. We thought
> he just wanted to shut us up, but we decided to go anyway.
> Were we ever surprised! He said that he and the board had
> been amazed at the response from parents, especially those
> who typically don't get involved in the district. He said he
> had had no idea the program was so popular. Then he asked

us to help him brainstorm other ways for the district to save money so that the program could continue.

The parents, together with some district staff, met for several weeks and came up with a solution that would save the district money and still keep the sports program alive. They proposed that local stores underwrite the operating expenses of the teams, and the school district would pay for the coaches and still save $150,000. Once the idea was approved, the parents helped recruit local merchants.

We know of parents who have organized for other purposes: to support the granting of tenure to a principal, to urge the initiation of shared decision making in their district, to demand the establishment of standards of excellence at the local high school, or to support a candidate running for a seat on the school board. Sometimes their campaigns have been as elaborate as the Smiths'; sometimes not. The most successful campaigns were those that were thoughtfully and passionately planned, that were assertive but not hostile, and that included a willingness to collaborate with schoolpeople, knowing that might mean some compromises.

ACCOUNTABILITY

With all the talk these days about accountability, it is surprising how little it is understood. Most educators and parents think that schools are held accountable through standardized test scores. Every year, one of the local newspapers publishes a rank ordering of all New York City public schools according to their students' reading scores, thinking that by making this information public, they are holding the schools accountable. And this is not unusual; it happens in other cities, too.

While test scores do provide a means for measuring student achievement—a flawed means, as we pointed out in Chapter 6—these and any other forms of assessment are not the same as accountability. Accountability happens only when action is taken as a result of the scores. In a truly accountable school, in other words, test scores are not simply reported and filed away. When test scores (or teacher and parent observations or class work or any other measure used) indicate that there is a problem, an accountable school tries to solve it.

A principal we knew used his school's reading scores in this way every year. He spent hours analyzing them in order to discern patterns; he looked at the children's scores by class and by grade and compared them with previous years' scores. Then he met individually with teachers to formulate plans. If a particular third-grade class showed a pattern of difficulties with reading comprehension, for example, the principal helped that teacher develop new techniques for emphasizing comprehension in her class. While we're not fans of standardized testing, this particular principal used the results to trigger an accountability system in his school.

The same kind of system can be activated for an individual child. In Chapter 6, we told you what Erica's mother and her teacher did when Erica's reading scores dropped. That was also accountability, begun in that instance by the parent.

Accountability can be a difficult topic to discuss with schoolpeople. Teachers sometimes get defensive, equating it with punishment. Their fear seems to be that if they don't achieve the desired results (that is, high enough reading scores), they will be called on the carpet. That isn't accountability any more than filing away test scores is. In an accountable school, a teacher having difficulties gets support, such as the way our principal friend helped teachers in his school.

Sometimes a school or district gets defensive, too, and seeks to hide shortcomings out of fear of parent recriminations or unfavorable publicity, rather than trying to find solutions in partnership with parents.

The schools are accountable to us and our children. Yes, we are responsible for our children's attendance and preparation, and our children are responsible for doing their work. But the school is accountable for our children's learning.

THE ACCOUNTABLE SCHOOL

- Has high expectations for children and staff
- Looks for ways to meet every child's needs and does not let any children fall through the cracks
- Looks at the whole child
- Adapts to children's learning styles rather than expecting children to fit a preconceived mold
- Uses curriculum and instructional practices that are developmentally appropriate
- Looks at children's strengths rather than their weaknesses
- Sets high standards for student achievement and provides the resources and supports needed to reach them
- Values the professional wisdom and experience of its staff
- Supports the professional growth of its staff
- Sees parents as partners, not adversaries
- Seeks parental input to help understand children
- Shares insights about children with their parents
- Respects the cultures and languages of its families
- Reports regularly and meaningfully to parents on their children's progress
- Seeks to solve problems rather than cover up or justify mistakes
- Has clearly defined goals, ways to assess its progress toward meeting them, and methods of reporting on that progress to the broader community

FURTHER READING

Ann Bastian et al. *Choosing Equality*. Philadelphia: Temple University Press, 1986.

Jill Bloom. *Parenting Our Schools: A Hands-on Guide to Education Reform*. Boston: Little, Brown, 1992.

Hispanic Policy Development Project. *Queridos Padres: La Escuela Es Nuestra Tambien (Dear Parents: It's Our School Too)*. New York, 1990.

Carl L. Marburger. *One School at a Time: School Based Management, A Process for Change*. Columbia, MD: National Committee for Citizens in Education, 1985.

Larry Martz. *Making Schools Better: How Parents and Teachers Across the Country Are Taking Action—and How You Can, Too*. New York: Times Books/Random House, 1992.

Donald Moore et al. *Standing Up for Children: Effective Child Advocacy in the Schools*. Chicago: Designs for Change, 1989.

National Committee for Citizens in Education, *Public School Choice: An Equal Chance for All?* Columbia, MD, 1989.

———. *Parents Organizing to Improve Schools*. Columbia, MD, 1985.

Jeannie Oakes and Martin Lipton. *Making the Best of Schools*. New Haven, CT: Yale University Press, 1990.

PARTING THOUGHTS

When we started to write this book, we couldn't imagine that we'd have enough words and stories to fill its pages. Now, two years and hundreds of hours later, we find it hard to stop—we have so much more to say!

In many ways, this has been a humbling experience. While we knew from the beginning that we didn't have all the answers, we did believe that we had been around long enough to be able to synthesize into concrete suggestions what we and others had observed and experienced over the years. It didn't turn out to be that simple. We had to rediscover what we already knew: Each of us has to find our own way to get involved and to advocate for our children.

Another thing we relearned along the way is how passionate we are about our beliefs and our approach to parent participation. You'll recognize the underpinnings of our book; we think they're worth repeating:

• We parents know our children better than anyone else. Because of that, we must make our voices heard

and participate in our children's educational experiences.
• We parents should trust our instincts about our children.
Our parenting and observation skills can help us confirm
that there is a problem brewing or that everything is okay.
• We parents have the power to influence our children's
school experiences. While we may not be able to remedy
every situation, our advocacy can usually improve it.
• We parents have to use our best judgment and then "wing
it." The approach that works with one teacher, one principal, or one child might not work with another. There are
no formulas.
• We parents can't do it alone. But only when goals and
expectations are shared with schoolpeople can we work as
partners. The critical ingredient, then, is *communication*.
• We parents need to be realistic about what we can and
cannot change so that we can focus our efforts and achieve
results. We also need to recognize that trade-offs and compromises are often necessary.
• We parents must always be mindful of how our actions
might affect other people's children. When we advocate for
better teaching, better curricula, or better assessment practices for our children, we improve the experiences of other
children, too—but only when we advocate for practices that
are inclusive rather than exclusive.

We hope we haven't led you to believe it's easy. It hasn't
been for us. When Diane's daughter needed help with her
research project as we struggled to meet deadlines on this
book, it wasn't easy. She had to find a way to do both.
Years ago, when Laurette's daughter was hurt by a teacher's careless comment or when her son was not placed in
an appropriate learning group, it wasn't easy, either.
Through her experience in the PTA, Laurette had learned
to react rationally rather than emotionally to school issues,

but when they hit home, all she wanted to do was protect her children. She, too, had to find a way to do both. While advocating for our children, we've had to compete against the reality of schools and classrooms that have as their goal the education of *all* children, not just our own. And we suspect that some of the dilemmas we've struggled with will also cause you pain and some sleepless nights.

We hope we haven't led you to believe that you can do it all. No one can. We can't be superparents, nor should we try. We remember evenings when we came home from work too exhausted to speak, only to have a child ask us for help with studying for a social studies test, with reviewing spelling words, or with difficult math problems. Sometimes, when we thought we couldn't move another muscle, we did. Sometimes we didn't, and our kids survived.

Above all, we want to leave you with the message that the rewards of your participation far outweigh the frustrations. While we can't take credit for every good grade or report well done, we know that our involvement has helped our children. In addition to the benefits to her children, Laurette's editorship of that very first newsletter led directly to completing her education, to her present-day job, and to this book. For Diane, a reward came when her daughter, then in fourth grade, marched on her own to the principal's office to advocate for herself and her classmates.

Finally, we do believe in the message we've given you: *You can make a difference in the quality of your child's education!* And that's the biggest and best reward of all.

RESOURCES

All of the following organizations offer publications, either free of charge or for a nominal fee. Some give advice to parents, and most also have lists of other resources. In addition, many also act as advocacy organizations on behalf of parents and children.

Academy for Educational Development
100 Fifth Avenue
New York, NY 10011
212-243-1110

American Association of School Administrators
1801 North Moore Street
Arlington, VA 22209
703-528-0700

ASPIRA Association, Inc.
National Office
1112 16th Street, N.W., Suite 340
Washington, DC 20036
202-835-3600

Association for Childhood Education International
11501 Georgia Avenue, Suite 315
Wheaton, MD 20902
301-942-2443

Association for the Gifted (TAG)
Council on Exceptional Children
1920 Association Drive
Reston, VA 22901
703-620-3660

Children's Defense Fund
122 C Street, N.W., Suite 400
Washington, DC 20001
202-628-8787

Educational Equity Concepts, Inc.
114 East 32nd Street
New York, NY 10016
212-725-1803

Family Math Program
EQUALS Program
Lawrence Hall of Science
University of California
Berkeley, CA 94720
510-642-1823

Family Science Program
Northwest EQUALS
Portland State University
Portland, OR 97207
800-547-8887, ext. 3045

Hispanic Policy Development Project
36 East 22nd Street, 9th Floor
New York, NY 10010
212-529-9323

Institute for Responsive Education
605 Commonwealth Avenue
Boston, MA 02215
617-353-3309

International Reading Association
800 Barksdale Road
P. O. Box 8139
Newark, DE 19714
800-336-READ

National Association for the Education of Young Children
1509 16th Street, N.W.
Washington, DC 20036
800-424-2460

National Association of Secondary School Principals
1904 Association Drive
Reston, VA 22091
703-860-0200

National Black Child Development Institute
1023 15th Street, N.W., Suite 600
Washington, DC 20005
202-387-1281

National Center for Fair and Open Testing (Fairtest)
342 Broadway
Cambridge, MA 02139
617-864-4810

National Coalition for Parent Involvement in Education
National Community Education Association
801 North Fairfax Street, Suite 209
Alexandria, VA 22314
703-683-6232

National Coalition of Advocates for Students
100 Boylston Street, Suite 737
Boston, MA 02116
617-357-8507

National Committee for Citizens in Education (NCCE)
10840 Little Patuxent Parkway, Suite 301
Columbia, MD 21044
800-NET-WORK
301-997-9300

National Congress of Parents and Teachers (PTA)
700 North Rush Street
Chicago, IL 60611
312-787-0977
and
2000 L Street, N.W., Suite 600
Washington, DC 20036
202-331-1380

National Council of La Raza
810 1st Street, N.E., Suite 300
Washington, DC 20002
202-289-1380

U.S. General Services Administration
Consumer Information Center
P. O. Box 100
Pueblo, CO 81002

Women's Educational Equity Act Publishing Center
Educational Development Center, Inc.
55 Chapel Street
Newton, MA 02160
800-225-3088